The 1994-95 Complete

#125
200

ANTIQUE SHOP DIRECTORY

for Eastern Michigan
and the Upper Peninsula

Listing All Known Shops and Malls
Days and Hours of Operation
Seasonal Changes in Hours
Telephone Numbers
Editor's Comments
Directions for Finding the Shops & Malls
Detailed Maps Showing Exact Locations
Recommended Points of Interest
Sources of Area Information
Index of Dealer Specialties
Antique Sho~

Published by
Edward Lawre∟
Complete Antique Shop ᴅ⌐ectories
P.O. Box 297
14906 Red Arrow Highway
Lakeside MI 49116
616 469-5995

D1711672

Table of Contents

Table of Contents - continued

INTRODUCTION

This Antique Shop Directory is intended to provide the serious antiquer with a valuable tool for making his or her antiquing trips more efficient and enjoyable.

Information on Each Shop & Mall
Unlike some directories that list only those shops and malls that pay to advertise, this Directory lists ALL antique shops that could be identified. Each listing contains the name of the shop or mall; the address; the telephone number; the days and hours of operation; seasonal variations; and a brief description of how to find the shop or mall.

Some of the antique shops and malls have a brief comment from the editor. Such comments were generally included for shops that have a specialty, and for shops that had a large number of gifts or reproductions.

Maps Showing Shop & Mall Locations
Another feature that makes this Directory unique is that the location of each shop and mall is shown on a map. These maps are indented only to show the general location of the shop, and should be used in conjunction with a more detailed street map.

Shops Not Included
Shops that were almost entirely gifts, crafts, used furniture, or reproductions were not included. Shops with gifts, crafts, used furniture, and reproductions were listed (and so noted in the editors comment) if they also had a significant number of antiques.

Order of Listings: By Tier By County
This Directory covers all the counties in Eastern Michigan and the Upper Peninsula, from the Ohio border on the south to Lake Superior on the north.

The listing of the shops and malls is organized as follows: the eastern portion of the Lower Peninsula has been divided into ten tiers of counties, each group consisting of a horizontal tier of counties extending half-way across the state from Lakes Huron, St. Clair, and Erie on the east, to the center of the state (roughly the counties containing U.S. Highway 27). The Upper Peninsula comprises the eleventh tier of counties. The eleven tiers are numbered from south to north. Tier Number One is adjacent to the

Ohio border; Tier Two lies just to the south, etc. Within each tier, counties are numbered from east to west.

Thus, each county can be identified with the number of the tier it is located in, and its sequence number within that tier. *In this directory a county numbering system with a decimal point is used. The number to the left of the decimal point is the tier number, counting from the south; the number to the right of the decimal point is the county sequence number within that tier, counting from the east.* Monroe County, at the southeast corner of the state, is in Tier One. Being the eastern-most county in that Tier, it has a county sequence number of one. Thus the identification number is 1.1 for Monroe County. Livingston County is in the 3rd tier of counties north of the Ohio border, and is the 3rd one in from the east; thus it has an identification number of 3.3.

Caution

The editor traveled the entire area in late 1993 and early 1994, visiting most of the shops or malls. Those not visited had the data verified by telephone. Efforts have been made to make this Directory as accurate and complete as possible. Antique shops do close and move, however, and new ones open. Also, dealers may change their hours.

The editor cannot be responsible for any inconvenience due to erroneous or outdated information. Users of this Directory should also be aware that the hours given are "targets" of the antique dealers. Sometimes dealers go to auctions, estate sales, or away on personal business, and may not be there at a time when they are normally open. Also, some dealers do shows on certain weekends. Please take this into account, and be considerate if this occurs. Almost all shops and malls are closed Christmas, and some are closed other holidays. It is always best to call if you intend to drive out of your way to visit a shop.

Additional Information Provided

For the convenience of users of this directory, phone numbers of chambers of commerce are provided as a source of information about most counties. For many counties recommended points of information are indicated. Many of these recommendations are from an excellent book: *Hunt's Highlights of Michigan*, by Mary and Don Hunt, published by Midwestern Guides.

Map of Eastern Michigan

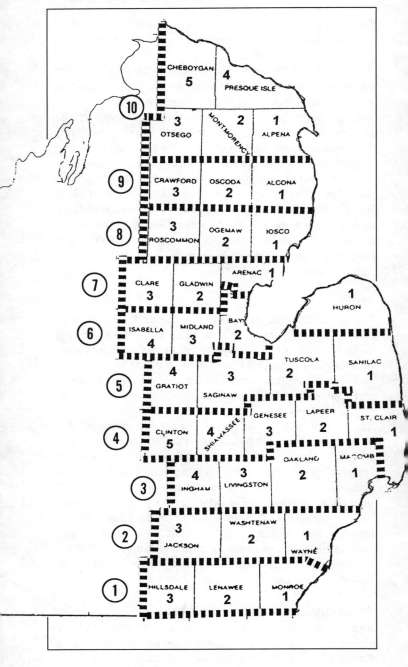

(8) Tier Number

4 County Sequence Number

6

Map of The Upper Peninsula

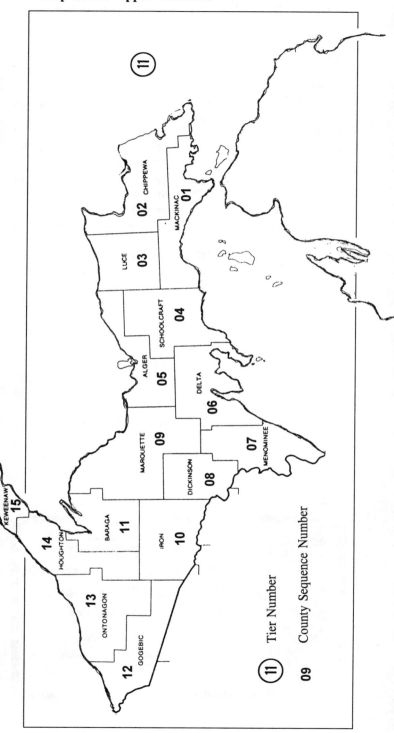

11   Tier Number

09   County Sequence Number

INDEX OF COUNTIES
(County, Tier & Sequence Number, and Page Number)

8

Index of Towns and Cities
(City, Tier & Sequence Number, County, Page Number)

Holly 3.21 Oakland	98	Onaway 10.4 Presque Isle .	199
Holt 3.4 Ingham	116	Onsted 1.2 Lenawee	20
Houghton Lk. 8.3 Roscn.	185	Oscoda 8.1 Iosco	181
Houghton 11.14 Houghton	227	Ovid 4.5 Clinton	140
Howell 3.3 Livingston . .	102	Owosso 4.4 Shiawassee . .	137
Imlay City 4.2 Lapeer . .	125	Parma 2.3 Jackson	64
Indian Rvr. 10.5 Cheboygan	201	Perry 4.4 Shiawassee . .	188
Iron Mntn. 11.08 Dickinson	215	Pinconning 6.2 Bay	168
Iron River 11.10 Iron . .	221	Plymouth 2.1 Wayne . .	42
Ironwood 11.12 Gogebic .	224	Pontiac 3.2 Oakland	91
Ithaca 5.4 Gratiot	158	Port Austin 6.1 Huron . .	163
Jackson 2.3 Jackson	62	Port Huron 4.1 St. Clair .	120
Jerome 1.3 Hillsdale	22	Port Sanilac 5.1 Sanilac . .	144
Johannesburg 10.3 Otsego	197	Prescott 8.2 Ogemaw . . .	184
Jonesville 1.3 Hillsdale . . .	23	Prudenville 8.3 Roscmn. .	185
Keego Harbor 3.2 Oakland	94	Ramsay 11.12 Gogebic . .	223
Kingston 5.2 Tuscola . . .	148	Reading 1.3 Hillsdale . . .	23
La Branche 11.07 Menmie.	215	Richmond 3.1 Macomb . .	69
Laingsburg 4.4 Shiawase. .	138	Rochester 3.2 Oakland . . .	90
Lake Orion 3.2 Oakland . .	91	Romeo 3.1 Macomb	72
Lake Linden 11.14 Houhtn.	227	Romulus 2.1 Wayne	48
Lakeport 4.1 Saint Clair . .	122	Roscommon 8.3 Roscmn.	187
Lansing 3.4 Ingham . . .	114	Royal Oak 3.2 Oakland . . .	77
Lapeer 4.2 Lapeer	126	Rudyard 11.02 Chippewa .	205
LaSalle 1.1 Monroe	11	Saginaw 5.3 Saginaw . . .	154
Leslie 3.4 Ingham	110	Saline 2.2 Washtenaw . . .	55
Lewiston 10.2 Montmcy. .	195	Sault S Marie 11.02 Chipwa.	204
Lexington 5.1 Sanilac . .	142	Snyder Lake 9.2 Oscoda .	191
Linden 4.3 Genesee	128	Somerset Ctr. 1.3 Hillsdale .	22
Livonia 2.1 Wayne	45	Somerset 1.3 Hillsdale . . .	22
Mackinaw 10.5 Cheboygan	201	South Lyon 3.2 Oakland .	96
Manchester 2.2 Washtenaw .	58	Southfield 3.2 Oakland . .	84
Manistique 11.04 Scholcft.	209	St. Clair 4.1 Saint Clair . .	119
Manitou Bch. 1.2 Lenawee .	21	St. Clair Shrs. 3.1 Macomb	67
Marine City 4.1 St. Clair .	118	St. Ignace 11.01 Mackinac	203
Marlette 5.1 Sanilac . . .	146	St. Johns 4.5 Clinton . . .	140
Marquette 11.09 Marqte. .	217	St. Louis 5.4 Gratiot . .	159
Marysville 4.1 St. Clair . .	120	Standish 7.1 Arenac . . .	174
Mason 3.4 Ingham	110	Stockbridge 3.4 Ingham . .	106
McMillan 11.03 Luce . .	207	Tawas City 8.1 Iosco . . .	180
Melvin 5.1 Sanilac . . .	146	Tecumseh 1.2 Lenawee . .	17
Memphis 3.1 Macomb . .	71	Trenton 2.1 Wayne	39
Menominee 11.07 Menmie.	215	Troy 3.2 Oakland	89
Merrill 5.3 Saginaw	157	Utica 3.1 Macomb	72
Midland 6.3 Midland . . .	169	Vassar 5.2 Tuscola	150
Millington 5.2 Tuscola . .	150	Warren 3.1 Macomb	71
Mio 9.2 Oscoda	190	Washington 3.1 Macomb . .	72
Monroe 1.1 Monroe	12	Waterford 3.2 Oakland . .	94
Mt. Clemens 3.1 Macomb .	68	Wayne 2.1 Wayne	47
Mt. Pleasant 6.4 Isabella .	171	Webberville 3.4 Ingham .	116
Munising 11.05 Alger . .	210	West Branch 8.2 Ogemaw	184
Negaunee 11.09 Marquette	218	Westland 2.1 Wayne . . .	46
New Baltimore 3.1 Macomb	68	Wheeler 5.4 Gratiot . . .	159
New Boston 2.1 Wayne . .	48	White Lake 3.2 Oakland .	94
Newberry 11.03 Luce . .	206	Whittemore 8.1 Iosco . . .	182
Northville 2.1 Wayne . . .	41	Williamston 3.4 Ingham . .	107
Oak Park 3.2 Oakland . . .	77	Wyandotte 2.1 Wayne . .	39
Okemos 3.4 Ingham . . .	112	Ypsilanti 2.2 Washtenaw . .	50
Omer 7.1 Arenac	174	Yale 4.1 St. Clair	123

TIER 1:
ALONG THE OHIO BORDER

1.1 MONROE COUNTY

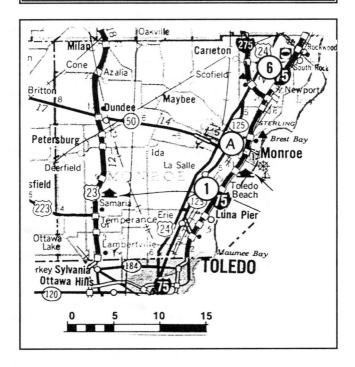

A. Monroe: 2 to 5 (See Detail Map)

Recommended Points of Interest:
1. Monroe: Loranan Square downtown historic district.
2. Monroe: Navarre Trading Post, N. Custer & Raisinville.

Additional Information:
Monroe County Chamber of Commerce, 313 242-3366

LASALLE

1 American Heritage Antique Mall
5228 S. Otter Creek Road, I-79 Exit 9
LaSalle, MI 48145
313 242-3430; FAX 313 242-3436
Every day 10 to 5
Northeast Corner I-79 & S. Otter Creek Road, 9 miles
north of the state line.

Detail Map: Monroe

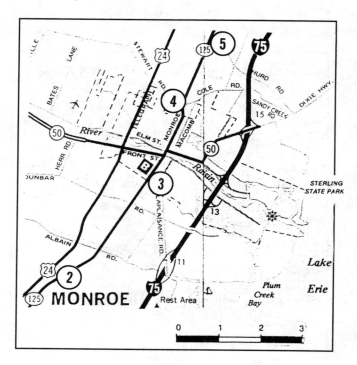

MONROE

2 Sauer Furniture & General Store
15300 S. Dixie Highway (M-125)
Monroe, MI 48161
313 242-6284
Tues. to Fri. 10 to 6, Sat. 10 to 5
I-75 to Exit 11 West 1 Mi. to Dunbar left 1 mi. to
M-125 left 1/4 mile.
Used furniture, some antiques.

3 Spainhower's Antiques
315 South Monroe
Monroe, MI 48161
313 242-5211
Mon. to Fri. 9 to 4
South of downtown, east side of street.
Mostly an auction house, but may have some antiques
for sale.

4 Lori's Treasures
476 North Monroe
Monroe, MI 48161
313 241-3287
Tues. to Fri. 10 to 6

5 Nichols Antiques
2784 North Monroe
Monroe, MI 48161
313 243-6666
By chance.
East side of highway.
Mostly an auction company, but may have some items
for sale.

CARLETON

6 Once Again
10200 Telegraph Road
Carleton, MI 48117
313 586-2240
Fri. to Sun. 10 to 5
U.S. 24, 1/4 mi. North of I-275, east side of highway.

1.2 LENAWEE COUNTY

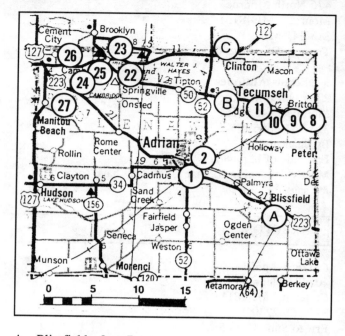

A. Blissfield: 3 to 7
B. Tecumseh: 12 to 15
C. Clinton: 16 to 21

Recommended Points of Interest:
1. Tecumseh: Hidden Lake Gardens; hiking trails,
conservatory, gardens. On M-50, 8 miles west of Tecumseh.
2. Clinton: 1942 Southern Michigan Railroad; 320 South
Division at Clark Street. 45 minute trip between Clinton and
Tecumseh. Weekends June to Sept. 517 456-7677

Additional Information:
Tecumseh Area Chamber of Commerce, 517 423-3740

ADRIAN

1 Marsh's Antique Mall
136 S. Winter Street
Adrian, MI 49221
517 263-8826
Mon. to Sat. 10 to 5, Sun. 1 to 5, closed Wed.
Downtown, west side of street between Maumee &
Church Streets, one block west of Main Street.

2 Adrian Antique Mall
122 N. Main Street
Adrian, MI 49221
517 265-6266
Mon. to Sat. 10 to 5:30, Sun. & most holidays 12 to 4
Downtown, east side of street between Toledo &
Maumee Streets.

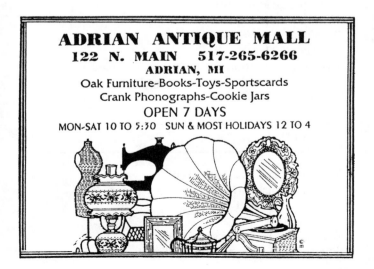

BLISSFIELD

3 Green's Gallery Of Antiques
115 South Lane Street
Blissfield, MI 49228
Days: 517 486-3080; Eves: 517 486-3025
Tues. to Sat. 10 to 5:30; Sun. 12 to 5:30
Downtown, 1/2 block south of light at U.S. 223.

4 Estes Antique Mall
116-118 South Lane,   Downtown
Blissfield, MI 49228
517 486-4616
Tues. to Sat. 10:30 to 5; Sun. 12 to 5

5 Blissfield Antique Mall
101 West Adrian Street (U.S. 223)
Blissfield, MI 49228
517 486-2236
Mon. to Sat. 10 to 5:30; Sun. 12 to 5
Downtown;   50 dealers

6 J & B Antiques Mall
109 West Adrian Street U.S. 223
Blissfield, MI 49228
517 486-3544
Mon. to Sat. 10 to 5:30; Sun. 12 to 5
Downtown;   52 dealers

7 Triple Bridge Antiques
321 West Adrian Street (U.S. 223)
Blissfield, MI 49228
517 486-3777
Mon. thru Fri. 10 to 5, Sun. 12 to 5, Closed Wed.
South side of road, just west of the bridge.
Parking in rear of store.

BRITTON

8 YesterYears Antique Mall
208 East Chicago (M-50)
Britton, MI 49229
517 451-8600
Winter: Sat. & Sun. 11 to 5:30;
Summer: Sat. & Sun. 12 to 5:30

𝔅ritton 𝔙illage 𝔄ntiques

132 E. Chicago (M-50) just west of RR tracks.
General line of antiques/collectibles.

(517) 451-8129

---

9 Britton Village Antiques
132 Chicago Blvd. (M-50)
Britton, MI 49229
517 451-8129
Summer: Thurs. to Sun. 10 to 5:30;
Winter Thurs. to Sun. 10 to 5
West of the tracks, downtown, south side of street.

10 Mckinney's Collectibles
108 East Chicago (M-50)
Britton, MI 49229
517-451-2155
Mon. to Fri. 2:30 to 6; Sat. 10 to 5, or by appointment.
World's largest beer can store.

TECUMSEH

11 L & M Antiques
7811 East Monroe Road (M-50)
Tecumseh, MI 49286
517 423-7346
Tues. to Fri. 12 to 5:30, Sat. & Sun. 11 to 5:30
3 miles east of Tecumseh.

12 Great Ideas
154 East Chicago Blvd. (M-50)
Tecumseh, MI 49286
517 423-6094
Mon. to Fri. 9 to 6:30, Wed. to 8; Sat. 9 to 5:30;
Sun. 12 to 4
East end of downtown, south side of the street.

13 Tecumseh Antique Mall I
112 East Chicago Blvd. (M-50)
Tecumseh, MI 49286
517 423-6441
Daily 10 to 5; Sun. 12 to 5
Downtown, south side of street.

14 Tecumseh Antique Mall II
1111 West Chicago Blvd. (M-50)
Tecumseh, MI 49286
517 423-6082
Mon. to Sat. 10 to 5; Sun 12 to 5
North side of M-50, west end of town.

15 Hitching Post Antique Mall
1322 East Monroe Road
Tecumseh, MI 49286
517 423-8277
Daily 10 to 5:30
2 miles West of Tecumseh. 40 dealers.

CLINTON

16 Clinton Antiques & Turn of the Century Lighting
116 West Michigan
Clinton, MI 49236
517 456-6019
Sat. & Sun. 10 to 6, other days: chance or appointment.
Downtown, north side of street.

17 Mainstreet Antiques
126 West Michigan Ave.
Clinton, MI 49236
517 456-7093
Mon. to Sun. 12 to 5
Downtown, north side of street.

18 Antiques Emporium
134 West Michigan (U.S. 12)
Clinton, MI 49236
517 456-6153
Daily 10 to 6
Downtown, north side of street.

19 The Wooden Box
141 West Michigan
Clinton, MI 49236
517 456-7556; 456-4794
Wed. to Sat. 12:30 to 5:30, or by appointment.
Downtown, south side of street.

20 The Rose Patch
162 West Michigan
Clinton, MI 49236
517 456-6473
Winter: Tues. to Sat. 10:30 to 5, Sun. 11 to 5
Summer: Mon. to Wed., Fri. & Sat. 10:30 to 5,
Sun. 11 to 5.
Downtown, north side of street.

21 Oak City
1101 West Michigan Ave.
Clinton, MI 49236
517 456-4444
Tues. to Sun. 10 to 6
South side of the highway.

1.2 Lenawee County - continued

ONSTED

22 Jerry & Sherry's Antiques
10487 M-50
Onsted, MI 49265
517 467-4885
Summer: Wed. to Sun. 10 to 6

BROOKLYN

23 Irish Hills Antiques
10600 US 12
Brooklyn, MI 49230
517 467-4646
"Good chance or appointment."
Set back on north side of highway, 1 mile east of M-50.
Specializing in antique wood and coal burning kitchen
and parlor stoves.

24 The Granite Rooster Antiques & Collectibles
12341 Pink Street (also Person Road)
Brooklyn , MI 49230
517 592-6307
May 1st to Labor Day: Every Day 11 to 5;
Spring & Fall: 12 to 6 by appointment.
Closed Dec. to Mar.
U.S. 12 & M-50
(Lower level Brick Walker Tavern.)

25 Brick Walker Tavern Antiques
11705 US-12
Brooklyn, MI 49230
517 467-4385
Summer: Wed.to Sat. 10 to 5, Sun. 11 to 5;
Winter: Thurs. to Sat. 10 to 5, Sun. 11 to 5
U.S. 12 & M-50, Cambridge Junction.
Three floors.

26 Muggsie's Antiques and Collectibles
13982 West U.S. 12
Brooklyn, MI 49230
517 592-2659
Fri. to Mon. 12 to 5
North side of U.S. 12, half mile west of Brooklyn Road
Glassware

MANITOU BEACH

27 Kellk's Curios
14013 Woerner
Manitou Beach, MI 49253
517 547-5482
Daily 12 to 5, closed Thurs. & Sun.
From U.S. 12 go south on U.S. 223 to Round Lake
Highway, take Round Lake Highway to Geneva, then
south to Woerner Street. Shop is at the corner of
Woerner & Hallenbeck Streets, south of Round Lake.
Glass, Flow Blue, primitives, jewelry, books.

MAP OF HILLSDALE COUNTY:

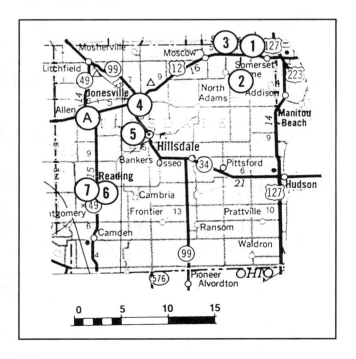

1.3 HILLSDALE COUNTY

MAP ON PRECEDING PAGE

A. Allen: 8 to 24

Recommended Points of Interest:
1. Jonesville: Grosvenor House Museum, 517 849-9596
2. Hillsdale: Slayton Arboretum, at Hillsdale College
Additional Information:
Greater Hillsdale Chamber of Commerce, 517 439-4341

SOMERSET

1 Summerset House
12465 Chicago Road (U.S. 12)
Somerset, MI 49282
517 688-9816
May to Oct. : Thurs. Fri. Sun. & Mon.: 11 to 4:30;
Sat. 9:30 to 6
South side of highway, 3 miles west of U.S. 127.

SOMERSET CENTER

2   Bob's Antiques
1261 Chicago Road (U.S. 12)
Somerset Center , MI 49282
517 688-3596
March to December: Wed. to Fri. 11 to 5; Sat. 8 to 5;
Winter: Weekends only.
South side of U.S. 12, 3 miles west of U.S. 127.

JEROME

3 Bundy Hill Truck Stop
9880 East Chicago Road (U.S. 12)
Jerome, MI 49269
517 688-4269
Summer: 24 hours Every Day;
Winter: 24 hours Fri. & Sat.; Sun. to Thur. 6 am 10 pm
North side of highway.
Small collectibles & antique shop in back of restaurant.

1.3   Hillsdale County - continued

JONESVILLE

4 Antiques
Northwest Corner Evans and North Streets
Jonesville, MI 49250
Telephone number & hours not available.
1 block north of Town Hall, east end of downtown.
The town allows no parking on any near-by street.

HILLSDALE

5 Carriage Anne Park Antique Mall
3390 Beck Road
Hillsdale, MI 49242
517 439-1815
Tues. to Sun. 10 to 6
Take M-99 south 3 miles from U.S. 12 to Beck Road;
west side of road.   Opened 1994.

READING

6 Gallaway and Swafford
122 South Main Street, downtown
Reading, MI 49274
517 283-3603
April thru October: Thurs. & Fri. 12 to 5, Sat. 10 to 5
November thru March: Sat. 10 to 5

7 The Finer Things
112 East Michigan
Reading , MI 49274
517 283-2451
By chance or appointment.
Downtown, 3 doors east of light, north side of street.
Glassware, clocks, pottery, furniture.

ALLEN

8   Grandpa's Attic Antiques
222 East Chicago
Allen , MI 49227
517 523-2993
Thurs. to Tues. 10 to 5.   East end of town.

9 1850's House Antiques, Collectibles, Crafts
113 East Chicago (U.S. 12)
Allen, MI 49227
No telephone listed.
Hours not available.
Blue house, east end of town, south side of highway.

10   A Horse of Course
U.S. 12 & Prentiss
Allen , MI 49227
517 869-2527
By chance
Northwest corner Prentiss & U.S. 12, east side of town.
Furniture in the rough & other antiques.

11   Michiana Antiques
100-104 West Chicago
Allen , MI 49227
517 869-2132
Summer: Every day 10 to 5; Winter: Every day 10 to 4
Northwest corner U.S. 12 & M-49, at the light.
Established 1967.

12   Hand & Hearts Antiques & Folk Carvings
109 W. Chicago
Allen , MI 49068
517 869-2553 (278-6485, 639-4891)
Summer: 12 to 5 every day except Wednesday;
Winter: Chance or appointment
Downtown, just west of light, south side of street.
Antiques and contemporary wood carvings.

13   Old Allen Township Hall Shops
114 West Chicago Road
Allen , MI 49227
517 869-2575
Every day 10 to 5
Downtown, north side of street.
12 dealers, 5,500 square feet.

14   Andy's Antiques
118 West Chicago Road
Allen , MI 49227
517 869-2182
Fri. to Wed. 10 to 5
Downtown, 4 doors west of light.

15   Poor Richard's Antiques & Rare Books
122 West Chicago Road
Allen ,   MI 49227
517 869-2637; 437-7449 res.
By chance
Downtown, just west of light, north side of U.S. 12.

16   J & Y Antiques
126 West Chicago Road
Allen ,   MI 49227
517 869-2289
Fri. to Sun. 10 to 6; Mon. to Thurs. by chance.
North side of street, west of light.

17   Timeless Treasures
West Chicago Road
returned by post office
Allen ,   MI 49227
517 869-2127
Sat. & Sun. 11 to 5; Mon. to Fri. by chance.
West of light, south side of U.S. 12.

18   Diggers of Antiques
151 West Chicago Road
Allen ,   MI 49227
517 869-2319; 517 849-9715
Summer: Fri. to Tues. 11 to 5; Wed. & Thurs. by
chance;   Winter: Fri. to Wed. 12 to 5
Downtown, one block west of light, south side of the
highway.

19   160 W. Chicago Antiques
160 West Chicago Road
Allen ,   MI 49227
517 869-2492
Every day 11 to 6
Downtown, west of light.
Crowded with Victorian furniture, glassware, and a
general line of antiques.

20   Peddlers Alley
162 West Chicago Road
Allen ,   MI 49227
517 869-2280 shop; 517 523-3741 home
Summer: Every day 11 to 5; Winter: closed Wed.
West side of town, north side of U.S. 12

21   The Village Peddler
164 West Chicago Road
Allen , MI 49227
517 869-2280 shop;   517 523-3741 home
Summer: Every day 11 to 5; Winter: closed Wed.
West side of town, north side of U.S. 12.
Glassware, jewelry, some furniture.

22   Olde Chicago Pike Antique Mall
211 West Chicago Road
Allen , MI 49227
517 869-2719
Summer: Every day except Wed. 11 to 6;
Winter: Every day except Tues. & Wed. 11 to 5.
West side of town, south side of U.S. 12.

23   Green Top Country Village Antique Mall
U.S. 12, 1/2 mile west of Allen
Allen , MI 49227
517 869-2100
Every day 10:30 to 5
1/2 mile west of Allen, south side of U.S. 12.
Complex of twenty historic structures; 65 dealers.
One of the dealers specializes in Mission Oak.

24   Allen Antique Mall
9011 West Chicago Road (U.S. 12)
Allen , MI 49227
517 869-2788
Mon. to Sat. 10 to 5; Sun. 12 to 5
Southwest corner U.S. 12 & Duck Lake Road, west end
of town.

See page 236 for the Index of Dealer Specialties.

TIER 2:
DETROIT TO JACKSON

2.11 WAYNE COUNTY
EASTERN PORTION

A. Grosse Pointe Area (See Detail Map)
B. Downtown Detroit (See Detail Map)
C. Mid-Town Detroit (See Detail Map)
D. Dearborn & Southern Suburbs (See Detail Map)

Recommended Points of Interest:
1. Detroit: Eastern Farmers' Market, I-75 to Mack Avenue.
Market days: Tues. and Sat. 313 833-1560
2. Detroit: Pewabic Pottery, 10125 East Jefferson (set back,
north side of the street.) 313 822-0954
3. Downtown Detroit: the People Mover system; the art deco
Guardian Building (Griswold & Congress); Silver's office

supply & gift store (151 West Fort at Shelby); Greektown & Trappers Alley (500 block of Monroe Street).

4. Dearborn: Greenfield Village, 20900 Oakwood Boulevard. 313 271-1620

5. Dearborn: Fair Lane (Henry Ford Estate), 4901 Evergreen Road. 313 593-5590

6. Grosse Pointe Shores: Edsel and Eleanor Ford House, 1100 Lake Shore Road. 313 884-4222

7. Fisher Mansion, 383 Lenox, 313 331-6740

Additional Information:
Metro Detroit Conv. & Vis. Bureau, 313 259-4333

Detail Map: Grosse Pointe Area

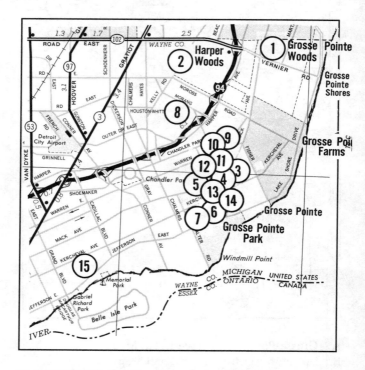

GROSSE POINTE WOODS

1 Calling House Antiques
20788 Mack
Grosse Pointe Woods, MI 48236
313 882-1652
Mon-Fri 9-4, Sat 9-3, Sun 9-12
East Side of the road, North of Vernier

HARPER WOODS

2 Peddler's Alley II
19354 Kelly
Harper Woods, MI 48225
313 526-7888
Mon. to Fri. 11:30 to 6, Sat. 10 to 5
West side of highway between 7 Mile & 8 Mile Roads

GROSSE POINTE

3 Danielle, Inc.
17009 Kercheval
Grosse Pointe, MI 48230
313 882-4101
Mon. to Sat. 10 to 5
Across from Jacobson's Department Store, 1/4 block
west of Notre Dame Street, north side of street.
Prints and Porcelain

4 Charterhouse & Co
16835 Kercheval
Grosse Pointe, MI 48230
313 885-1232
Mon. to Fri. 9 to 5
North side of street, 1/2 block east of Cadieux.
High quality estate jewelry, silver, autographs, etc.

GROSSSE POINTE PARK

5 Heirloom Accent
15227 Kercheval
Grossse Pointe Park, MI
Vi: 313 882-1108; Jerry: 313 833-5509
Wed. to Sat. 11 to 6
North side of street, 1/2 block west of Beaconsfield.
Antiques, jewelry, used furniture, collectibles.

6 Lloyd Davis Antiques
15302 Kercheval
Grosse Point Park, MI 48230
313 822-3452
Mon. & Wed. to Sat. 11 to 6
South side of street.

7 Grosse Pointe Reliques
14932 Kercheval
Grosse Pointe Park, MI 48230
313 822-0111
Wed. to Sat. 11 to 5:30 or by appointment
Between Alter & Wayburn near Detroit border.

DETROIT

8 Mike's Antiques
11109 Morang
Detroit, MI 48207
313 881-9500
Mon. to Sat. 10 to 6, Sun. 12 to 4
From I-94 Cadieux exit, west three blocks; south side of
street.

9 Ports Of Call Ltd.
16434 East Warren
Detroit, MI 48224
313 884-9779
Wed. to Sat. 12:30 to 5:30 or by appointment
North side of street, west of Cadieux. Across from Old
Algier Theatre.

10 Arthur Anderson Antiques
16422 East Warren Avenue
Detroit, MI 48224
313 886-6180
By appointment.
North side of street, west of Cadieux.

11 The Village Peddler
16358 East Warren
Detroit, MI 48224
313 882-3598
Tues. to Sat. 10 to 5
Southeast side of street, 1 block east of Outer Drive.

12 The Mahogany Furniture Source
16135 Mack Avenue
Detroit , MI 48224
313 886-1916
Wed. to Sat. Noonish to 5
North side of street, west of Cadieux.

13 Another Time
16239 Mack Avenue
Detroit, MI
313 886-0830
Wed. to Sat. 12 to 5
North side of street, west of Cadieux.

14 Park Antiques
16235 Mack Avenue
Detroit, MI
313 884-7652
Wed. to Sat. 12 to 5
North side of street, west of Cadieux

15 William Charles Gallery
8025 East Agnes
Detroit, MI 48214
313 823-0324
Mon. to Fri. 4 to 7, Sat. & Sun. 10 to 6, or by
appointment.
From downtown: east on Jefferson to Van Dyke, north
on Van Dyke two blocks, east on Agnes.

16 Marketplace Gallery
2047 Gratiot
Detroit, MI 48207
313 567-8250
Tues. Thurs. & Fri. 1 to 6, Sat. 9 to 6
Northwest side of street, 1/2 block northeast of Vernor,
at St. Alban Street.
High quality antiques.

17 Dell Pryor Galleries
1452 Randolph
Detroit, MI 48226
313 963-5977
Tues. to Sat. 11 to 5, or by appointment
East side of downtown. East side of Randolph, a block
north of Gratiot, across from a little park in the
Harmonie Park Historic District. The lower level has
high quality antiques, the upper level has 4 art
exhibitions per year.

Detail Map: Downtown Detroit

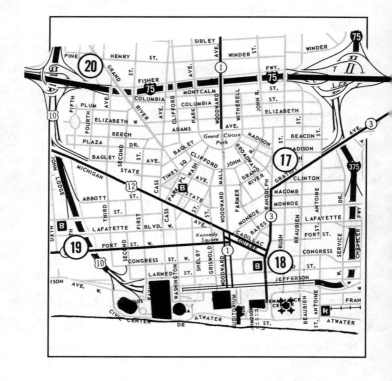

The line on the map circling downtown is the monorail
people-mover system; it offers both good transportation
and a great view of downtown.

18 DuMouchelle Art Gallery
409 East Jefferson
Detroit, MI 48226
313 963-6255
Mon. to Fri. 9:30 to 5:00, Sat. 9:30 to 5
Downtown, north side of street across from Renaissance
Center.
High quality ornate antiques; auctions.

19 John L. King Books
901 West Lafayette Blvd.
Detroit, MI 48226
313 961-0622
Mon. to Sat. 9:30 to 5:30
Just west of downtown, south side of street, west of
Lodge Expressway.
Huge used book store, plus small room of antiques.

20 Detroit Antique Mall & Senate Resale
828 West Fisher Freeway North-side Frontage Road
Detroit, MI 48201
313 963-5252
Tues. to Sat. 11 to 6
Northwest of downtown. North side of entrance ramp to
Fisher Freeway, just west of Grand River Avenue.
(There is a street to avoid entering the freeway after
leaving the mall.)
Large interesting mixture of antiques and used furniture.

21 Xavier's
2546 Michigan Avenue
Detroit, MI 48216
313 964-1222
Tues., Thurs., & Fri. 11 to 5, Sat. 10 to 6
5 blocks west of Tiger Stadium.
Mission, Art Deco & Moderne furniture and Accessories

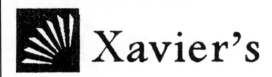

Detail Map: Mid-Town Detroit

22 Gallery Of Antiques
7105 Michigan
Detroit, MI 48226
313 554-1012
Tues. to Sat. 10 to 6
South side of street.

23 New World Antique Gallery
12101 Grand River
Detroit, MI 48204
313 834-7008
Mon. to Sat. 11 to 6
Southwest side of street, west of Wyoming at Washburn.
Building full of antiques and used furniture, much of it
in the rough.

24 Northwind Antiques
16331 West Warren
Detroit, MI
313 582-1931
By chance.
Southwest corner Westwood & Warren, midway
between Telegraph and Greenfield.
Small shop with collectibles & antiques.

25 Teem Antiques
19403 West Warren
Detroit, MI 48228
313 336-2121
By chance or appointment.
4 blocks east of Evergreen.

HAMTRAMCK

26 Peddler's Alley
3630 Caniff
Hamtramck, MI 48212
313 872-1813
Mon. to Sat. 11:30 to 7, closed Thurs.
West of Conant Avenue.

DEARBORN

27 ACE Jewelry & Coins
13840 Michigan
Dearborn, MI 48126
313 584-7430
Mon. to Sat. 9 to 6
South side of street at Maple Street light.

28 Retro Image
14246 Michigan
Dearborn, MI 48126
313 582-3074
Mon. to Sat. 11 to 7
Between Schaffer and Greenfield
1920's to 1950's, etc.

Detail Map: Dearborn & Southern Suburbs

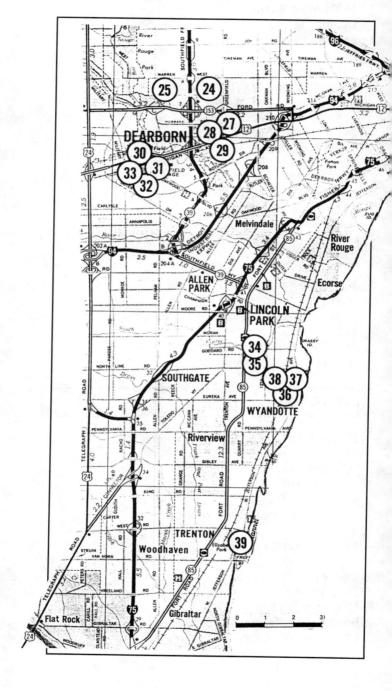

29 Desirable Discs II
13939 Michigan Ave.
Dearborn, MI 48126
313 581-1767
Mon. to Thur. 10 - 9; Fri. & Sat. 10 - 10; Sun. 12 - 6
South side of street, 1 block west of Maple Street light.
Vintage records, posters, books, music memorabilia.

30 Howard Street Antiques
921 Howard
Dearborn, MI 48124
313 563-9352
Mon. to Fri. 10 to 6, Sat. 10 to 4, Sun. by appointment.
From Michigan & Military go east on Michigan to 1st
light, north on Howard 1/2 block, east side of street.

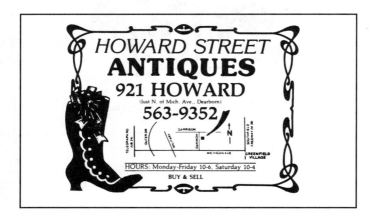

31 Comer-Copia
21903 Michigan
Dearborn, MI 48126
313 565-0875
Mon. to Sat. 10 to 5
Southwest corner Michigan & Oakwood.

32 Rancho House
22027 Park Avenue
Dearborn, MI 48120
313 563-3705
Tues., Thurs. to Sat. 9 to 5, Wed. 9 to 12
1 block south of Michigan Avenue, west of Maple
Street.
Beauty shop with some antiques.

33 Village Antiques
22091 Michigan Ave.
Dearborn, MI 48124
313 563-1230
Mon. to Sat. 10:30 to 5:30; Sun. 12 to 5; Thurs. to 7:30
South side of street, west of Monroe Street.
5,000 square feet; 35 dealers; antiques, collectibles,
jewelry, advertising, military, toys.

Quality Furniture & Accessories • Buying One Piece or Entire Estate

WYANDOTTE

34 J & J Antiques
1669 Fort Road
Wyandotte, MI 48192
313 283-6019
Tues. to Sat. 10 to 5
East side of highway, north of North Line Road.

35 Tony's Junk Shop
1325 Fort Road
Wyandotte, MI 48192
313 283-2160
Summer: Mon. to Sat. 11 to 7;
Winter: Mon. to Sat. 9 to 7
Between North Line & Goddard

36 Yesterday's Treasures
258 Elm Street
Wyandotte, MI 48192
313 283-5232
Mon. to Fri. 10 to 5, Sat. 10 to 3

37 Etcetera Antiques
99 Oak
Wyandotte, MI 49192
313 282-3072
Mon. to Sat. 11 to 6; in summer also open Sun.
First & Oak Streets

38 Old Gray House Antiques
303 Oak
Wyandotte, MI 48192
313 285-2555
Mon. to Sat. 10 to 4
At Oak & Third Streets.

TRENTON

39 Don's Antiques & Collectibles
2857 West Jefferson
Trenton, MI 48183
313 676-0622
Mon. to Sat. 9:30 to 5
1/2 block south of West Road, east side of the street

2.12 WAYNE COUNTY
WESTERN PORTION

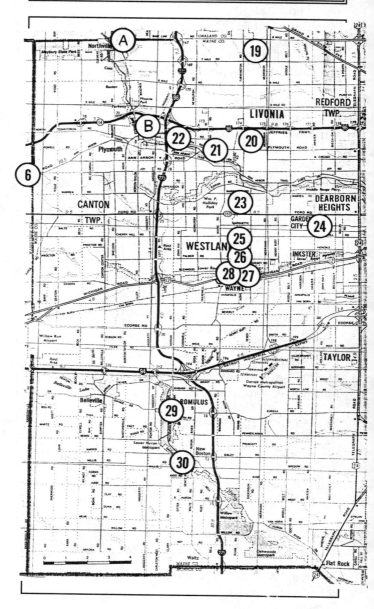

A. Northville: 1 to 5
B. Downtown Plymouth: 7 to 11 (See Detail Map)
C. Old Village Area, Plymouth: 12 to18

NORTHVILLE

1 Helen Meisel Antiques
320 North Center
Northville, MI 48167
810 349-9339; Res.: 313 474-6099
By appointment only.
North of downtown, east side of street behind the
Sawmill furniture barn.

2 La Belle Provence
119 North Center
Northville, MI 48167
810 347-4333
Mon. to Sat. 10 to 5, Sun. 12 to 4
West side of the street, just north of the downtown stop
light.
Antiques, gifts, fabric, new furniture.

3 McGuires Antiques & Fine Art
341 East Main Street
Northville, MI 48167
810 348-5550
Mon. to Sat. 12 to 8
3 blocks east of Downtown, north side of street.

4 Morrison's Antiques
105 East Main Street
Northville, MI 48167
810 348-8898
Tues. to Thurs. 11 to 4; Fri. & Sat. 10 to 5; Sun. &
Mon. by chance
3 doors East of Sheldon Road (i.e. Center Street).

5 Sherwood Picture Framing Antiques & Art
107 East Main Street
Northville, MI 48167
810 347-4890
Tues. to Fri. 10 to 6, Sat. 10 to 5, Mon. by Chance.
Second floor, above Morrison's Antiques, north side of
the street.

PLYMOUTH

6 The Shop Around
9885 West Ann Arbor Road
Plymouth, MI 48170
313 455-2920
Sat. & Sun. 12 to 5
From Exit 15 of M-14 south 1.5 miles to Plymouth Ann
Arbor Road, west 1/2 block, north side of road.

7 In My Attic
865 Wing
Plymouth, MI 48170
313 455-8970
Wed. & Sun. 12 to 6, Thurs. to Sat. 11 to 6
South side of the street, just west of Main Street, two
blocks south of downtown.
Antiques, collectibles, miscellaneous this & that items.

8 Jack's Corner Bookstore
583 West Ann Arbor Trail
Plymouth, MI 48170
313 455 2373
Tues., Wed., Fri. & Sat. 10:30 to 5
Downtown, 1 1/2 blocks east of Main Street, south side
of the street.
Antiquarian books and antiques.

9 Memory Lane Antiques
336 S. Main
Plymouth, MI 48170
313 451-1873
Mon. to Thurs.& Sat 11 to 5; Fri. 11 to 8; Sun. 12 to 5
Downtown, west side of street half block north of Ann
Arbor Trail, across from Kellogg Park

10 Burton Gallery Antiques
842 Penniman
Plymouth, MI 48170
313 451-1850
Mon. to Sat. 11 to 5 or by appointment.
Downtown, north side of street, just west of Main
Street.

Detail Map: Plymouth

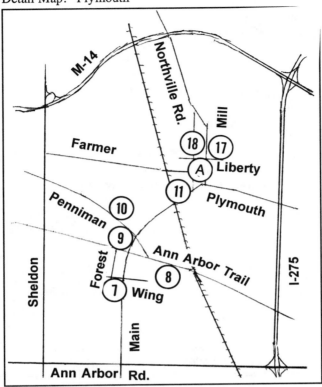

A. Liberty Street: 12 to 16

11 The Michael Camp Shoppe
331 North Main Street
Plymouth, MI 48170
313 453-0367
Mon. to Fri. 10 to 4; Sat. 11 to 5
West side of street, just north of tracks.

12 Upstairs, Downstairs Antiques
149 Liberty
Plymouth, MI 48170
313 459-6450
Tues. to Sat. 11 to 5, Sun. 12 to 5. Coop shop

13 Lady K's
181 Liberty
Plymouth, MI 48170
313 453-8975
Mon. to Sat. 10 to 6, Mon. & Thurs. to 9

14 Pritchard Antiques
187 Liberty
Plymouth, MI 48170
313 459-3442
Mon. to Sat. 11 to 5

15 Plymouth Antiques "Mini Mall"
195 Liberty
Plymouth, MI 48170
313 455-5595
Mon. to Sat. 11 to 6; Sun. 12 to 5
Corner of Liberty & Starkweather.
5,000 square feet; 9 dealers. Hunting & fishing items.

16 M. Hubert & Co. Antiques
198 W. Liberty (at Starkweather)
Plymouth, MI 48170
810 344-4725
Mon. to Sat. 11 to 5 or by appointment
5 blocks north of Ann Arbor Tr., 2 bks. west of Main.

17 Country Clutter
790 North Mill
Plymouth, MI 48170
313 455-3108
By appointment only.
White house, east side of street, just north of Liberty.

18 Mother-in-Law's Attic Antiques
748 Starkweather
Plymouth, MI 48170
313 454-4088
Wed. to Sun. 11 to 5
West side of street just north of Liberty.

LIVONIA

19 Now 'N' Then
33200 Seven Mile Road
Livonia, MI 48152
313 476-0055
Mon. to Sat. 11 to 5, Sun. 12 to 5
North side of the Street, 1 block east of Farmington Rd.
Gifts, jewelry, collectibles, antiques.

20 Town & Country Antiques Mall
31630 Plymouth Road
Livonia, MI 48150
313 425-4344
Mon. to Sun. 11 to 6 except holidays.
1 block west of Maramon Road, 1 mile south of I-96,
behind American Made Restaurant. 48 dealers

21 Countryside Craft Mall & Antiques
35323 Plymouth Road
Livonia, MI 48150
313 513-2577
Mon. to Sat. 10 to 6, Thurs. to 8; Sun. 12 to 5.
West of Wayne Road, south side of highway.
Crafts to the right, antiques to the left.

22 Plymouth Antique Emporium/Warehouse
38291 Schoolcraft Road, Suite 102
Livonia, MI 48150
313 591-3131
Call for an appointment.
Between Eckles and Newburg St.; Service Drive I-96

WESTLAND

23 Somewhere In Time
35948 Ford Road
Westland, MI 48185
313 729-7041
Tues. to Sat. 11 to 5
5 blocks west of Wayne Road, north side of street.
Parking lot entered from Walton Street east of shop.

Antiques and
Collectibles from:

Somewhere In Time

35948 Ford Rd.
Westland, MI 48185
(313) 729-7041

NANCY DZBANSKI
MARIE HARRIS

GARDEN CITY

24 Garden City Collectibles, Inc.
27821 Ford Road
Garden City, MI 48135
313 525-5155
Tues. to Sat. 10:30 to 6
Southwest corner Deering & Ford Road, set back in 2-
store mini-mall.
Small shop with stamps, coins, military items, antiques.

WAYNE

25 Vicky's Antiques & Resale
3019 Wayne
Wayne, MI 48184
313 728-3101
Mon. to Fri. 11 to 5, Sat. 11 to 6 Sun. by chance.
East side of street, 4 blocks north of U.S. 12; park and
enter in the rear.

26 Olde North Village Antiques
2903 Wayne Road
Wayne, MI 48184
313 722-0145
Summer: Tues. to Sun. 10 to 6; Winter: Wed. to Sun.
10 to 6
Southeast corner Glenwood & Wayne Road, 1 mile
north of U.S. 12.

27 Blue Willow
34840 West Michigan (West-bound lanes.)
Wayne, MI 48184
313 729-4910
Mon. to Sat. 11 to 6, Sun. 12 to 5
North side of street, 1 block west of Wayne Road.

(313) 729-4910

BLUE WILLOW ANTIQUES INC.

34840 MICH. AVE. WEST
WAYNE, MI 48184

28 Sanders Antiques
35118 West Michigan (West-bound lanes.)
Wayne, MI 48184
313 721-3029
Every day 10 to 6
North side of the street, 1/4 block west of Wayne Road.

ROMULUS

29 Santaland Antiques
16060 Hannan Road
Romulus, MI 48174
313 941-5555
Wed. to Sun. 11 to 5
West side of street, 1.6 miles south of Wabash.
Multi-Dealer Shop.

NEW BOSTON

30 Country Squire Antiques Mall
19232 Huron River Drive
New Boston, MI 48164
313 753-3820
Tues. to Sun. 11 to 5; Fri. to 6
Just north of the downtown stop light, west side of
street.

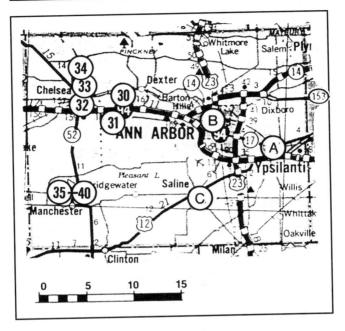

A. Ypsilanti: 1 to 7 (See Detail Map)
B. Ann Arbor: 8 to 21 (See Detail Map)
C. Saline: 22 to 29 (See Detail Map)
D. Manchester: 35 to 40

Recommended Points of Interest:
1. Ann Arbor: Kelsey Museum of Archaeology, 434 South State Street. 764-9304
2. Ann Arbor: Univ. of Michigan Museum of Art, 525 South State at South University. 313 764-0395
3. Ann Arbor: Stearns Collection of Musical Instruments, School of Music, at the end of Baits Drive. 313 763-4389
4. Ann Arbor: Hands-On Museum, 219 East Huron, 313 995-KIDS.
5. Ann Arbor: Ehnis & Son, 116 W. Liberty, old time clothing store.
6. Ypsilanti: Miller Motors, 100 East Cross; 1940's Hudson dealership. 313 482-5200
7. Manchester: Historic downtown with 1820's gristmill, blacksmith shop, 150 year-old library, harpsichord factory, etc.

Additional Information:
Ann Arbor Convention & Visitors Bureau: 313 995-7281
Manchester Area Chamber of Commerce: 313 428-7722

YPSILANTI

1 McFarlane Antiques
10970 Ford Road (M-153)
Ypsilanti, MI 48197
313 482-1307
Tues. to Sun. 12:30 to 5:30
From Exit 10 of M-14 go east on M-153 4 miles; south side of road.
Specializing in cut & pressed glass

Detail Map: Ypsilanti

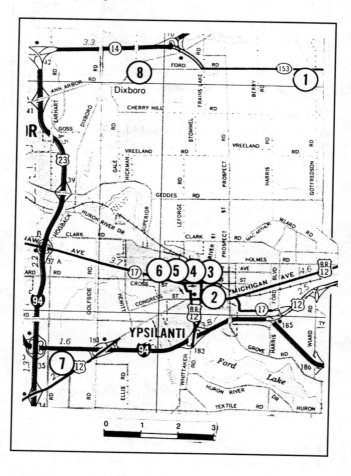

2 Materials Unlimited
2 West Michigan Avenue
Ypsilanti, MI 48197
313 483-6980; Fax 313 482-3636
Tues. to Sun. 10 to 5
Downtown, north side of street just west of the river.
Antique and new architectural items, & antiques.
Parking in the rear.

3 Cross Street Mall
33 East Cross Street
Ypsilanti, MI 48197
313 482-4525
Tues. to Sun. 11 to 5
Depot Town District (4 blocks north of downtown),
north side of street.

4 Jim MacDonald's Antiques & Apple Annies Vintage Clothing
29 East Cross Street
Ypsilanti, MI 48198
313 481-0555
Tues. to Sat. 11 to 5:30, Sun. & Mon. 12 to 4
Depot Street Historic District, north side of street.
Two shops share the same building.

5 Winding River Originals
23 East Cross Street
Ypsilanti, MI 48197
313 483-3133
Tues. to Sat. 10 to 6, Sun. 12 to 5
North side of street.
Antiques and local 2D and 3D art gallery.

6 Remington Walker Design Associates
19 East Cross Street
Ypsilanti , MI 48197
313 485-2164
Fri. 6 to 9 p.m.; Sat. 10 to 5; Sun. 1 to 5; or by
appointment.
North side of street.
Interior design and antiques.

7 Schmidt's Antiques
5138 W. Michigan
Ypsilanti, MI 48197
313 434-2660
Mon. to Sat. 9 to 5, Sun. 11 to 5
1 mile west of I-94, between Ypsilanti & Saline, north side of highway.

ANN ARBOR

8 Gibbons
5135 Plymouth Road
Ann Arbor, MI 48105
313 663-2277
Mon. to Sat. 11 to 5; Sun. 1 to 4
North side of street, just east of Dixboro, 1.5 miles east of U.S. 23
Vintage buttons, paper advertising, etc.

9 Antiques Mall of Ann Arbor
2739 Plymouth Road
Ann Arbor, MI 48103
313 663-8200
Mon. to Sat. 11 to 7, Sun. 12 to 5
North side of road in Plymouth Road Mall shopping center, located between Huron Parkway and Nixon Road. Enter from an alcove under the "China Merchandise" sign.   40 dealers.

10 The Treasure Mart
529 Detroit Street
Ann Arbor, MI 48104
313 662-9887
Mon. to Sat. 9 to 5:30
Northeast of downtown; north side of street between Fifth Ave. & Division Street.
Three crowded floors of consignment household goods.

11 Barrett's Antiques & Fine Art
212 East Washington
Ann Arbor, MI 48104
313 662-1140
Thurs. to Sat. 11 to 7, or by appointment.
South side of street between Fourth & Fifth Avenues,
Excellent collection of art pottery.

Detail Map: Ann Arbor

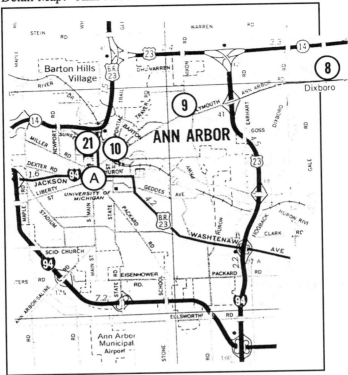

A. Downtown Ann Arbor: 11 to 20

Note: In downtown Ann Arbor park at one of the large
parking garages (Ann & Ashley and William & Fourth); bring
lots of quarters.

12 Art Deco Design Studio
207 East Washington
Ann Arbor, MI 48107
313 663-3326
Tues. to Sat. 11 to 5:30
North side of street.
Art Deco period items.

13 The Lotus Gallery
207 East Washington
Ann Arbor, MI 48104
313 665-6322
Tues. to Fri. 11 to 5:30, Sat. 11 to 5
East of 4th Avenue.
Oriental antiques and Southwestern American Indian art.

14 Past Presence Antiques
303 South Division
Ann Arbor, MI 48104
313 663-2352
Mon. to Sat. 11 to 6
SEC Liberty & Division
European & American antiques

15 Arcadian Antiques & Collectibles
13-15 Nickels Arcade
Ann Arbor, MI 48104
313 994-3433
Mon. to Sat. 10 to 5, Sun. 11 to 5
The historic Arcade is located on the east side of
Maynard Street between William and Liberty Streets.

16 Grace's Select Second Hand
122 South Main Street
Ann Arbor, MI 48104
313 668-0747
Mon. to Sat. 11 to 9
Downtown.

17 Barclay Gallery
218 South Main
Ann Arbor, MI 48104
313 663-2900
Tues. to Thurs. 11 to 7, Fri. & Sat. 11 to 9, Sun. 12 to
5
Downtown, west side of the street between Liberty &
Washington.

18 Arcadian Too
322 South Main Street
Ann Arbor, MI 48104
313 994-8856
Mon. to Thurs. 11 to 6, Fri. 11 to 9, Sat. 10 to 9, Sun.
12 to 6
Downtown, west side the street, south of Washington.

19 Rage Of The Age
220 South Fourth Ave.
Ann Arbor, MI 48107
313 662-0777
Tues. to Sat. 12 to 6
Vintage clothing & jewelry; 1950's items.

20 The Antique Store
305 South Ashley
Ann Arbor, MI 48104
313 930-0442
Wed. to Sat. 12 to 5
Downtown, Southeast Corner Liberty & Ashley.

21 Mac Gregor's Outdoors, Inc.
803 North Main
Ann Arbor, MI 48104
313 761-9200
Mon. to Sat. 10 to 6
Northwest corner Main & Summit, north of downtown.
American and European antique furniture
Antique Fly Fishing accessories.

SALINE

22 Antique International Interiors
405 North Ann Arbor Street
Saline, MI 48176
313 944-3500
Mon. to Sat. 10 to 5:30
North of downtown, west side of the street.
Interiors and antiques.

23 The Drowsy Parrot, Ltd.
105 North Ann Arbor
Saline, MI 48176
313 429-8595
Every day 7 a.m. to 10 p.m.
Downtown, west side of the street; also a restaurant.

24 Saline House Antiques Mall
116 West Michigan Ave.
Saline, MI 48176
313 429-5112
Mon. to Sat. 10 to 5; Sun. 11 to 5
Downtown
19 dealers.

Detail Map: Saline

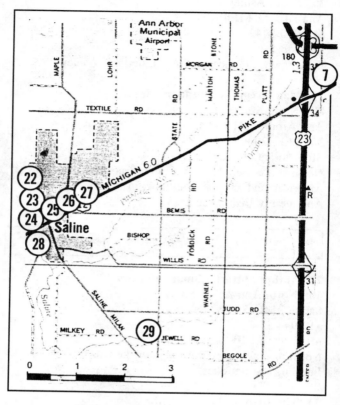

25 Pineapple House Interiors
101 East Michigan
Saline, MI 48176
313 429-1174
Mon. to Sat. 10 to 5; April to Dec. also open Sun. 12 to 4.
Downtown
Interior design, decorative items, new furniture, some antiques.

26 Great Ideas
105 East Michigan
Saline, MI 48176
313 429-1991
Mon. to Sat. 10 to 5, Sun. 12 to 4
Downtown
Antiques and interior design.

27   Saline Crossings
107 East Michigan Ave.
Saline, MI 48176
313 429-4400
Mon. thru Sat. 10 to 5; Sun. 12 to 4
Downtown, north side of street.

28   The Village Loft
109 West Michigan Ave.
Saline, MI 48176
313 429-7390
Mon. to Sat. 10 to 5; Sun. 12 to 4;
also April to Nov.: 3rd Sun. 9 to 5
Downtown
Multi-dealer shop.

29   Attic Treasures
10360 Moon Road
Saline, MI 48176
313 429-4242
Wed. to Sun. 11 to 5
West side of the road between Judd & Jewel Roads.

DEXTER

30   Glenbrier Antiques
351 N. Dancer Road
Dexter, MI 48130
313 475-2961
Every Day 10 to 6
Quarter mile north of Jackson Road; use Exit 162 from
I-94 eastbound, and Exit 167 from I-94 westbound. The
building to the right has the second best collection of old
tools in Michigan; the building straight ahead has mostly
glass and pottery.

31   Johnson's Antique Shop
11511 Jackson Road
Dexter, MI 48130
313 475-1902; 313 769-3848
Thurs. to Sunday 9:30 to 5 or by appointment. Closed
Jan. & Feb.
A mile east of I-94 Exit 162, south side of highway, at
Lima Center Road.

CHELSEA

32 Fireside Antiques
1196 South Main Street (M-52)
Chelsea, MI 48118
313 475-9390; Res. 313 475-7113
Thurs. & Fri. 12 to 5, Sat. 10 to 5, or by appointment.
1/4 mile north of I-94 Exit 159, west side of street.

33 Uptown Antiques & Littlewares
114 N. Main Street
Chelsea, MI 48118
313 475-6940
Summer: Mon. to Sat. 10 to 5:30; Winter Wed. to Sat.
12 to 5:30
North end of downtown, east side of the street.

34 Chelsea Woodwork & Antiques
407 North Main Street
Chelsea, MI 48118
313 475-8020
Fri. & Sat. 10 to 5, Sun. 12 to 4
North of downtown, just north of the tracks.

MANCHESTER

35 Antiques Etcetera
230 East Main Street
Manchester, IN 48158
313 428-9040
Wed. to Sat. 10 to 5, Sun. 12 to 5
Northwest Corner M-52 & Main Street.
Opened 1993.

36 Calamity Jane's
109 East Main Street
Manchester, IN 48158
313 428-1122
Mon. to Sat. 10 to 5, Sun. 12 to 5
Downtown, just east of Clinton, next to Post Office.

37 Raisin Valley Antiques
201 East Main Street
Manchester, MI 48158
313 428-7766; res. 313 428-8518
Tue. to Sat. 10 to 5, Sun. 12 to 5
Downtown, in the Mill.

38 Limpert Antiques
201 East Main Street
Manchester, MI 48158
313 428-7400
By appointment only, or by chance.
Downtown, lower level Manchester Mill.
Advertising, Civil War, etc.

39 Manchester Antique Mall
116 East Main Street
Manchester, MI 48158
313 428-9357
Every Day 10 to 5 (except Christmas, New Years, &
Thanksgiving day)
Downtown

40 The 18th Century Shoppe
122 East Main Street
P.O. Box 557
Manchester, MI 48158
313 428-7759
Wed. to Sat. 10 to 5, Sun. 12 to 5
Downtown, north side of street.
Country wares, herbs, gifts, antiques.

See the calendar of Antique Shows starting on page 230.

2.3 JACKSON COUNTY

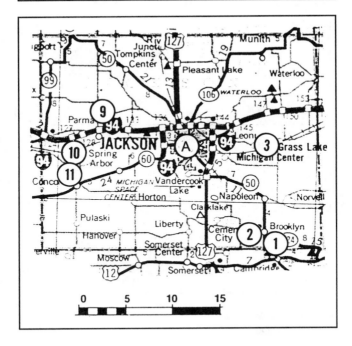

A. Jackson: 4 to 8 (See Detail Map)

Recommended Points of Interest:
1. Jackson: Ella Sharp Museum, 3225 4th St. 1855 Victorian Farmhouse, log house, school, & gardens. 517 787-2320
2. Jackson: Michigan Space Center, 2111 Emmons Road. 517 787-4425

Additional Information:
Jackson Conv. & Visitors Bureau, 517 783-3330

BROOKLYN

1   Brooklyn Depot Antiques
207 Irwin Street
Brooklyn , MI 49230
517 592-6885
Summer: Fri. & Sat. 11 to 5, Sun. 12 to 4;
Winter: Sat. 11 to 5, Sun. 12 to 4; best to call for appointment.
A block east of M 50, south side of town.
Bells, office furniture, etc.

2 Pinetree Centre Antique Mall
129 North Main Street
Brooklyn, MI 49230
517 592-3808
Mon. to Sat. 10 to 5, Sun. 12 to 5
Downtown, on the Square, east side of the street.

GRASS LAKE

3 Grand Illusion
103 & 201 East Michigan
Grass Lake , MI 48240
517 522-8715; 517 522-5822
Mon. to Sat. 9:30 to 4:30, Sun. 12 to 4
Downtown, south side of street.
Architectural salvage, art, jewelry.

JACKSON

4 Browse & Bargain
1361 E McDevitt
Jackson , MI 49203
517 782-5101
Daily 9 to 6
Intersection 127 & M-50. Used furniture, some antiques.

The Jackson Antique Mall, Inc.

201 N. Jackson Street
Jackson, Michigan 49201
(517) 784-3333

Monday - Saturday 10:00 - 6:00
Sunday 12:00 - 5:00

Detail Map: Jackson

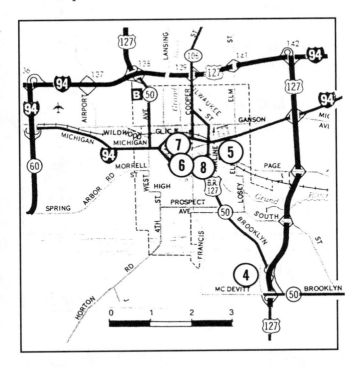

5 Cash 'n Carry
817 E. Michigan
Jackson , MI 49203
517 782-3167
Mon. to Fri. 9 to 6; Sat. 9 to 5; Sun. 10 to 5
East of downtown, south side of street.
Mostly used furniture, but some antiques.

6 Glory Days Antiques
171 West Michigan
Jackson, MI 49201
517 787-9193
Tue. to Fri. 9 to 5; Sat. 9 to 3; Sun. 12 to 4
Downtown, southeast corner Michigan & S. Jackson.

7 The Jackson Antique Mall
201 N Jackson St
Jackson , MI 49201
517 784-3333
Mon to Sat: 10 to 6; Sun. 12 to 6
Northeast corner Pearl & Jackson Streets, downtown.
40 dealers.

8 The Antique Shop
340 Otsego Street
Jackson, MI 49201
517 787-2033
Mon. to Fri. 8 to 5, Sat. 8 to 12
North side of Otsego just east of Washington, the one-way east-bound downtown loop street.
Western half of electric parts store.

PARMA

9. Cracker Hill Antique Mall
1200 Norton Road
Parma, MI 49269
517 531-4200
Mon. to Sat. 11 to 5; Sun. 12 to 5
Exit 128, north side of I-94.   26 dealers.

10 Harley's Antique Mall
13789 Donovan Road
Parma , MI 49224
517 531-5300
Every day except Christmas 10 to 6.
I -94 Exit 127, southwest corner.
12,000 square feet; opened 1992.

CONCORD

11 King Road Granary
12700 King Road
Concord, MI 49237
517 524-6006
April to Dec.: Wed. to Sun. 10 to 6
South from I-94 Exit 127 on West Concord Road 3.5
miles to King Road, west 1/2 mile; barn in back of
house, north side of road.

MICHIGAN'S WELCOME CENTERS...
A source for maps and travelers information

1. Ironwood: U.S. 2
2. Iron Mountain: U.S. 2
3. Menominee: U.S. 41
4. Marquette: U.S. 41
5. Sault Ste. Marie: I-75
6. St. Ignace: I-75
7. Mackinaw City: M-108

8. Clare: U.S. 27
9. Port Huron: I-94
10. Monroe: I-75
11. Dundee: U.S. 23
12. Coldwater: I-69
13. New Buffalo: I-94

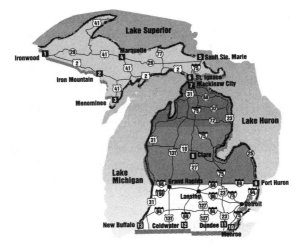

TIER 3:
NORTH OF DETROIT

3.1 MACOMB COUNTY

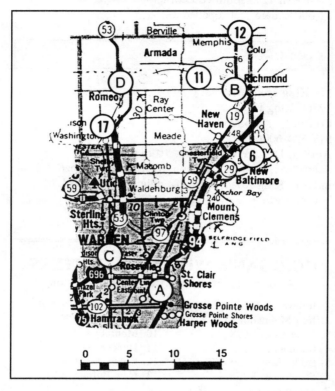

A. Southeast Macomb County: 1 to 5 (See Detail Map)
B. Richmond: 7 to 10
C. Southwest Macomb Co.: 13 to 16 (See Detail Map)
D. Romeo: 18 to 27

Recommended Points of Interest:
1. St. Clair Shores: Three lakeside parks, one of which contains the Selinsky-Green Museum, an 1860 log house.
2. Mount Clemens: Michigan Transit Museum, 200 Grand. 810 463-1863
3. Mount Clemens: Selfridge Military Air Museum, Eastbound I-94 to Exit 240, 2 miles east on Hall Road. 313 466-5035   Open April through October.

Additional Information:
Central Macomb County Chamber of Comm., 810 463-1528.

Detail Map: Southeast Macomb County

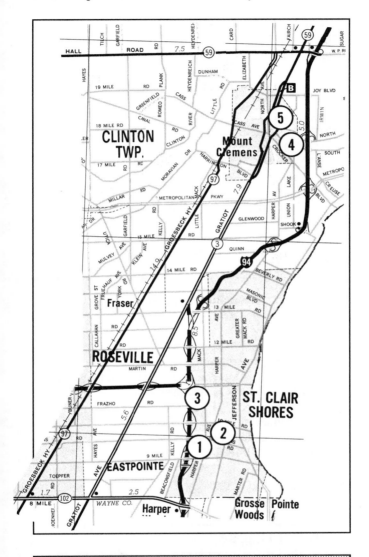

ST. CLAIR SHORES

1 Adams Antiques
19717 Nine Mile Road
St. Clair Shores, MI 48080
810 777-1652
Mon. to Thurs. 9 to 5, Fri. 9 to 8, Sat. 10 to 4
6 blocks w. of Harper, east of I-94, north side of road.
Very large shop; lots of English furniture.

2 Motor City Specialty Automotive
24440 Harper
St. Clair Shores, MI 48081
810 779-5353
Mon. to Fri. 10 to 5, Sat. 10 to 1, Wed. to 9
East side of street between 9 and 10 Mile Roads.
Antique auto parts and supplies.

3 Toodles
26717 Little Mack
St. Clair Shores, MI 48081
810 772-0920
Mon. to Sat. 9:30 to 2:30
West from Harper on 11 Mile Road, south on Little
Mack; west side of street in back of Victoria Place
Restaurant.

Mt. CLEMENS

4 Heather & Shamrock Antiques
24557 North River Road
Mt. Clemens, MI 48043
810 954-0011
Daily 10 to 6, closed Mon.
North side of the street, between Gratiot and I-94 Exit
237. In River Bend Center business mall.

5 Millers Place
Northeast corner East Scott & Gratiot Streets
Mt. Clemens, MI 48043
No telephone listed.
By chance.
Northeast of downtown.

NEW BALTIMORE

6 Heritage Square Antique Mall
36821 Green Street (M-29)
New Baltimore, MI 48047
810 725-2453
Tues. to Sat. 10 to 5; Sun 11 to 5
Northeast of downtown on M-29 past the light, north
side of street in a large white mansion.
20 dealers

RICHMOND

7 Sherry's at Richmond Interiors
67690 Main (M 19)
Richmond, MI 48062
810 727-9628
Tues. 11 to 5, Thurs. & Fri. 11 to 6, Sat. 11 to 5
East side of street, in a white house with bluegreen trim
attached to Richmond Interiors.
Gifts and antiques.

8 Lou Capp
68286 South Main Street (M-19)
Richmond, MI 48041
No telephone.
Mon. to Sat. 9 to 5
Yellow brick building just north of the tracks, at bend in
highway south of downtown. There is no sign.
Large building of used furniture, collectibles, and
antiques.

9 Wagon Wheel Antiques
69273 Main Street
Richmond, MI 48062
810 727-7474
Tues. to Fri. 10 to 3, Sat. & Sun. 10 to 5
Downtown, north of Division Street, west side of Main.

SHERRY'S ANTIQUERY
80515 S. Main Street (M-19)
Memphis MI 48041
We sell antiques, gifts, dolls, teddy bears,
and home accessories.   We specialize in
Country and Victorian antiques.
Also: visit our shop at Richmond Interiors,
67690 Main Street in Richmond.

Detail Map: Southwest Macomb County

10 Barb's Antique Mall
69394 Main Street (M-19)
Richmond, MI 48062
810 727-2826
Tues. to Sun. 12 to 5
North end of downtown, 3 blocks north of Division
Street, east side of street.   Antiques and crafts.

11 High Bank Antiques
28689 Armada Ridge Road
Richmond, MI 48062
810 784-5302
Summer: Fri. to Sun. 12 to 5, Tues. 10 to 2;
Winter: Fri. to Sun. 12 to 5
House on north side of highway, midway between
Richmond and Armada

MEMPHIS

12 Sherry's Antiquery
80515 South Main Street (M 19)
Memphis, MI 48041
810 392-2989
Thurs. to Sat. 11 to 5, or by chance or appointment.
West side of street, south of Bordman Road.
Antique Furniture, and gifts.

WARREN

13 Fred's Antique Furniture & Antiques
14091 8 Mile Road
Warren, MI 48089
810 776-7100
Mon. to Sat. 10 to 6, Sun. 11 to 5
North side of the street, 7 blocks west of Gratiot.
Used furniture, some in the rough; some antiques.

14 Silver Quill Antiques
22813 Van Dyke
Warren, MI 48089
810 756-8180
Mon. Tues. Fri. & Sat. 12 to 6, Sun. 1 to 6
West side of street, 2 blocks south of Nine Mile Road.
Glass, china, pottery, jewelry, etc.

15 Sterling Antiques
22835 Van Dyke
Warren, MI 48089
810 756-5923
Fri. to Tues. 12 to 6
Sun. 12 to 5
South of Nine Mile Road, west side of street.

UTICA

16 Bear Lair
7759 Auburn Road
Utica, MI
810 731-2894
Mar. to Dec.: Mon. to Sat. 10 to 6, Sun. 12 to 4;
Jan. & Feb.: Mon. to Sat. 11 to 5, Sun. 12 to 4
Downtown, north side of street, just west of Cass St.
light.
Gifts, dried flowers, antiques & collectibles.

WASHINGTON

17 Bank of Antiques
58415 Van Dyke (M-53)
Washington, MI 48094
810 781-5647; 810 798-3283
Tues. to Sun. 11 to 5
1/2 mile north of 26 Mile Road, west side of street.
Specializing in architectural antiques.

ROMEO

18 A Matter of Taste
105 South Main
Romeo, MI 48065
810 752-5652
Tues. to Sat. 11 to 5, Thurs. to 8; Sun. 12 to 5
Downtown

19 The Village Barn
186 South Main
Romeo, MI 48065
810 752-5489
Winter: Mon. to Sat. 10 to 5:30, Sun. 12 to 5:30;
Summer: Mon. to Sat. 10 to 6, Sun. 12 to 6
2 blocks south of the downtown light near the Hess
Manor Bed & Breakfast Inn, west side of street.
Cooperative, 4 dealers.

20 Seekers International Ltd.
247 East Lafayette
Romeo, MI 48065
810 752-8971; 313 524-0598
Thurs. to Sun. 10 to 6
1 block south of 32 Mile Road, 1.5 blocks east of Van
Dyke.
Antique architecture; imported English antiques and
collectibles.

21 Remember When Antiques & Collectibles
143 West St. Clair
Romeo, MI 48065
810 752-5499
Tues. to Thurs. & Sat. 10:30 to 5:30; Sun. 12 to 4
White house 2 blocks west of Main, south side of street.
A general line, specializing in glassware & china of the
Depression Era.

22 Town Hall Antiques
205 North Main
Romeo, MI 48065
810 752-5422
Daily 10 to 6
Downtown, west side of street just north of the light at
32 Mile Road.
50 dealers

23 Romeo Antique Mall
218 North Main Street
Romeo, MI 48065
810 752-6440
Mon. to Sat.10 to 6, Sun. 12 to 6
Downtown, northeast side of Old Van Dyke
Opened 1993; 20 dealers.

24 Harris Street Antiques
222 North Main
Romeo, MI 48065
810 752-9860
Mon. to Sat. 11 to 5
Downtown, east side of street.
Antiques & folk art.

25 Carriage Trade Antiques
264 North Main
Romeo, MI 48065
810 752-7778
Tues., Wed., Thurs. & Sat. 12 to 5
Blue house, southeast corner of Dickenson Street, 2
blocks north of the downtown light at 32 Mile Road.

26 Windmill Pointe Antiques
11731 29 Mile Road
Romeo, MI 48065
810 752-7259
Thurs. to Sun. 11 to 5
West of M-53, north side of road.

27 The Barn
M-37
Romeo, MI 48065
No telephone listed.
May to Oct.: Sat. & Sun. 10 to 5
West of Van Dyke, north side of road.

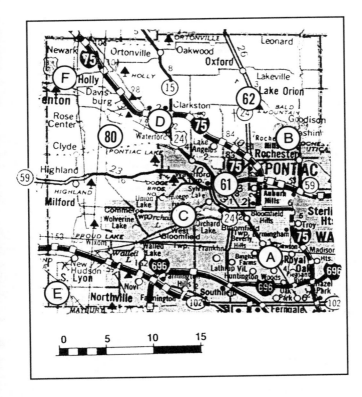

A. Southeast Oakland County: 1 to 55 (See Detail Map)
B. Rochester: 56 to 60
C. So. Central Oakland Co.: 63 to 71 (See Detail Map)
D. Clarkston: 72 to 76
E. South Lyon: 77 to 79 (See Detail Map)
F. Holly: 81 to 85

Recommended Points of Interest:
1. Bloomfield Hills: Cranbrook House and Gardens, 380 Lone Pine Road; April to Oct. 810 645-3149
2. Bloomfield Hills: Cranbrook Institute of Science, & Academy of Art Museum; 500 Lone Pine Road. 313 645-3312
3. Holly: Historic Holly Hotel, 110 Battle Alley. Restaurant in 1891 building. 313 634-5208
4. Royal Oak: Detroit Zoo, Woodward Avenue & Ten Mile Road. 810 398-0903
5. South Lyon: Railroad Museum, Cider Mill, Sawmill, etc.

Additional Information:
Oakland County Chamber of Commerce, 810 683-4747

Detail Map: Southeast Oakland County

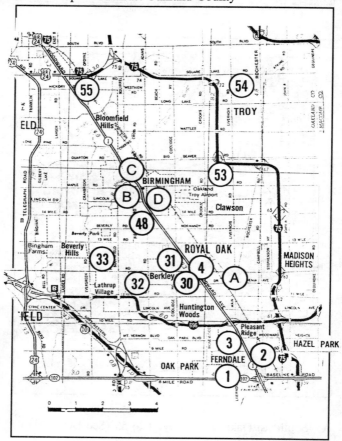

A. Downtown Royal Oak: 5 to 29
B. Downtown Birmingham: 34 to 40
C. North Woodward Avenue, Birmingham: 41 to 47
D. South Adams Square Bldg., Birmingham: 49 to 52

FERNDALE

1 Butterfly Shoppe Studio
637 Livernois
Ferndale, MI 48220
810 541-2858
Mon. to Wed. 10:30 to 4, Thurs. 10:30 to 7
Livernois is first major street west of Woodward; west
side of street between 8 and 9 Mile Roads.
Antique repair; some antiques.

2 Sally Wright Antiques
22446 Woodward
Ferndale, MI 48220
810 399-0339
Mon. to Sat. 11 to 5
East side of street, 2 blocks south of 9 Mile Road.
Old and reproduction lamps; stained glass windows.

OAK PARK

3 Neat Stuff
8558 West Nine Mile Road
Oak Park, MI
810 544-3026
Tues. to Fri. 12 to 6, Sat. 10 to 5
North side of the street; parking lot entrance from
Roanoke Street to the east.
Glasssware, smalls.

ROYAL OAK

Note: Most shops in Royal Oak are open the three
Sundays before Christmas.

4 Heritage Company II Architectural Artifacts
2612 N. Woodward
Royal Oak, MI
810 549-8342
Wed. to Sat. 11 to 5
East side of street between 12 and 13 Mile Roads.

5 Antique Connection
710 East Eleven Mile Road
Royal Oak, MI 48067
810 542-5042
Tues. to Sun. 10 to 5
South side of the road.

6 Ann's Fifth Avenue Antiques
110 East Fifth
Royal Oak, MI 48067
810 398-6697
Tues. to Sat. 12 to 6, Sun. by appointment
Downtown, south side of street, just east of Main Street.

9-5 Daily (7 days)   **(313) 543-0272**

𝕿𝖗𝖔𝖞 𝕾𝖙𝖗𝖊𝖊𝖙 𝕬𝖓𝖙𝖎𝖖𝖚𝖊𝖘
"We Buy and Sell Estates"

309 S. Troy St. Royal Oak, MI. 48067

Marty Tomaselli   **Ed Tomaselli**

7 Troy Street Antiques Mall
309 South Troy Street
Royal Oak, MI 48067
810 543-0272
Every day 9 to 5
East side of street, north of East Fourth Street.
Toys, Dolls, Jewelry, etc.

8 Daniel's Gallery of Antiques
412 East Fourth Street
Royal Oak, MI 48067
810 545-3990
Mon. to Sat. 12 to 6, Sun. 11 to 3, Wed. by chance
Downtown, south side of street
Lamps, glass, pottery, art

9 Grandma's Good-Stuff
405 East Fourth Street
Royal Oak, MI 48067
810 543-2335 or 810 548-1650
Mon. to Sat. 12 to 5, Sun. 11 to 5
North side of street.

10 Phoenix Stained Glass Works
325 East Fourth Street
Royal Oak, MI 48067
810 398-2840
Wed. to Fri. 10 to 6, Sat. 11 to 4
North side of street

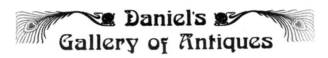
11 The Dandelion Shop
114 West Fourth Street
Royal Oak, MI 48067
810 547-6288
Mon. to Sat. 12 to 5
Downtown, north side of street between Center & Main
Antiques and decorative items.

12 Decades
110 West Fourth Street
Royal Oak, MI 48067
810 546-9289
Mon. to Sat. 11:30 to 5:30, Sun. 12 to 4
Downtown, north side of street

13 Duke Gallery
312 West Fourth Street
Royal Oak, MI 48067
810 547-5511; FAX: 810 547-5513
Mon. to Wed., Fri. & Sat. 11 to 6
Thurs. 11 to 9, Sun. 12 to 4
Downtown, north side of street in Washington Square
Plaza Building.
20th Century decorative arts, Mission Oak furniture

14 Deco Doug
106 West Fourth Street
Royal Oak, MI 48067
810 547-3330
Mon. to Sat. 12 to 6
Downtown, North side of street
Art Deco; Fifties

15 Antique Shoppe
309 South Main Street
Royal Oak, MI 48067
810 545-9060
Tues. to Fri. 11 to 6, Sat. 10 to 5, Sun. 12 to 5
Downtown, east side of street

16 Antiques on Main
115 South Main Street
Royal Oak, MI 48067
810 545-4663
Mon. to Sat. 10 to 6
Downtown, east side of street

17 Main Exchange
107 South Main Street
Royal Oak, MI 48067
810 546-9420
Mon. to Wed. 10 to 6, Thurs. 10 to 8, Sun. 12 to 5
Downtown, east side of street, south of 11 Mile Road.
Jewelry, glass, China, etc.

18 Mahogany Interiors
506 South Washington
Royal Oak, MI
810 545-4110
Mon. to Sat. 11 to 5:30, closed Wed.
Downtown, west side of street

**405 NORTH MAIN
ROYAL OAK, MI
(810) 542-6464**

a full range of antique
and vintage objects,
from furniture to
buttons which are our
specialty.

Monday thru Saturday 11-5

19 Lulu
405 North Main Street
Royal Oak, MI 48067
810 542-6464
Mon. thru Sat. 11 to 5.
Downtown, west side of street, north of 11 Mile Road.
Specializing in vintage and antique items from furniture
to buttons -- buttons an area of specialty.

20 Rare Old Prints
516 South Washington
Royal Oak, MI 48067
810 548-5588
Mon. to Sat. 11 to 6;
closed July, Aug., & 1st 3 weeks of Feb.
Downtown, west side of street

21 Vertu Deco and Fifties
511 South Washington
Royal Oak, MI 48067
810 545-6050
Tues. to Sat. 12 to 5
Downtown, east side of street

22 Decorative Arts 20th Century
415 South Washington
Royal Oak, MI 48067
810 398-0646
Mon. to Sat. 12 to 4:45
Downtown, east side of street
1930's to 50's designer furniture & accessories

23 Dave's Comics & Collectibles
407 South Washington
Royal Oak, MI 48067
810 548-1230
Mon. & Tues. 11 to 8, Wed. to Fri. & Sun. 11 to 5,
Sat. 11 to 7
East side of the street, just south of Fourth Street.
Comics, toys.

24 Yellow House Antiques
125 North Washington
Royal Oak, MI 48067
810 541-2866
Tues to Sat. 11 to 5, Sun. 12 to 5
West side of street, north of 11 Mile Road
11 dealers

25 North Washington Antiques
433 N. Washington
Royal Oak, MI 48067
810 398-8006
Mon. to Sat. 11 to 5
West side of street, north of 11 Mile Road

26 Del Giudice Gallery
515 South Lafayette Street
Royal Oak, MI 48067
810 399-2608
Mon. to Sat. 11 to 6
Downtown, 1 block west of Washington, Northeast
Corner Sixth & Lafayette.   Art and estate furniture.

27 Jeff Fontana Designs
500 West Eleven Mile Road
Royal Oak, MI 48067
810 543-8370
Mon. to Fri. 11:30 to 5, Sat. 12 to 4
Downtown, Northwest Corner West St. & 11 Mile Road
Design studio & European antiques & accessories.

28 Hauser Antiques
704 West Eleven Mile Road
Royal Oak, MI 48067
810 399-7650
Mon. to Fri. 11 to 6, Sat. & Sun. 10 to 5
North side of road, west of railroad tracks.

29 White Elephant Antique Shop
724 West Eleven Mile Road
Royal Oak, MI 48067
810 543-5140
Tues. through Sat. 11 to 5
North side of street, west of railroad tracks.

BERKLEY

30 Vanishing America
2965 West 12 Mile Road
Berkley, MI 48072
810 398-9420
Tues. to Sun. 11 to 4
Downtown Berkley, south side of the street, just east of
Robina Street.

31 Twice Around Resale Shop
2966 West 12 Mile Road
Berkley, MI 48072
810 545-6600
Tues. to Sat. 12 to 4
Downtown Berkley, north side of the street, just east of
Robina Street.
Glassware, used items, some antiques.

32 Doll Hospital & Toy Shoulder Shop
3947 West 12 Mile Road
Berkley, MI 48072
810 543-3115
Mon. to Sat. 10 to 5:30, Fri. to 8
South side of the street, 3 blocks east of Greenfield.
Dolls & toys, some antique.

SOUTHFIELD

33 The McDonnell House
19860 West 12 Mile Road
Southfield, MI 48076
810 559-9120
Mon. to Fri. 10 to 6; Sat. 9 to 5
Just east of Evergreen, north side of road.

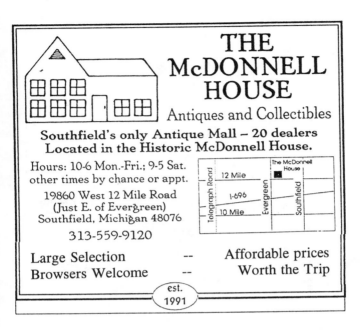
BIRMINGHAM

34 Trumbull's Antique Emporium
218 East Merrill
Birmingham, MI 48011
810 647-6833
"Open 7 days." (You may want to call first on Sun.)
South side of street, just west of Woodward. Downstairs,
below restaurant.
Opened 1993

35 Second Story Vintage Wristwatches
124 S. Woodward
Birmingham, MI 48011
810 642-1356
By appointment.
Second floor, west side of street, just south of Maple.

Detail Map: Downtown Birmingham

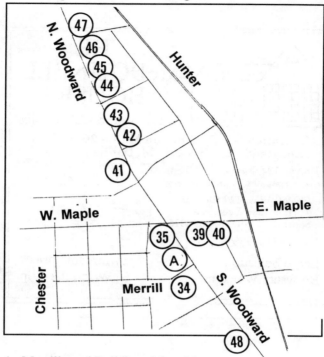

A. Merrillwood Building: 36 to 38

36 Edna Tillman Antiques
251 East Merrill
Birmingham, MI 48009
810 433-3746
Mon. to Sat. 11 to 4
Mezzanine level of Merrillwood Building, 1 block south
of Maple Road, northwest corner of Woodward.

37 Leonard Barry Antiques
251 East Merrill
Birmingham, MI 48011
810 646-1996
Mon. to Sat. 11 to 4
Merrillwood Building.

38 Chase Antiques
251 East Merrill
Birmingham, Mi 48009
810 433-1810; 810 543-4511
Mon. to Sat. 10 to 4
Merrillwood Building.

39 Watch Hill Antiques
330 East Maple
Birmingham, MI 48009
810 644-7445
Mon. to Sat. 10:30 to 5:30, Thurs. to 8
South side of street between Woodward and Hunter.
Country antiques and accessories from Europe.

40 L'Esprit
340 East Maple
Birmingham, MI 48011
810 646-8822
Summer: Mon. to Sat. 10 to 6;
Winter: Mon. to Sat. 10 to 5:30
South side of street between Woodward and Hunter.

41 The Hampton House Ltd.
523 North Woodward
Birmingham, MI 48011
810 645-2433, or 810 645-2434
Mon. to Sat.
West side of street, just north of Harmon.
Antiques and interiors.

42 O' Susannah, don't you cry for me
540 N. Woodward Avenue
Birmingham, MI 48009
810 642-4250
Tues. to Sat. 11 to 6, Thurs. until 8
East side of street.
Architectural artifacts, country primitives, gifts, etc.

43 Merwins Antique Gallery
588 N. Woodward
Birmingham, MI 48011
810 258-3211
Tues. to Sat. 12 to 5, but call ahead.
East side of street, just south of public metered parking
lot.   Small shop.

44 Chelsea Antiques
700 North Woodward
Birmingham, MI 48009
810 644-8090
Tues. to Sat. 10 to 5:30
Next to Joie De Vie Antiques.

45 Joie De Vie
700 North Woodward
Birmingham, MI 48009
810 644-8448
Mon. to Sat. 10 to 5
East side of street, just south of Vinewood.
French country antiques & accessories.

46 Madeline's Antique Shop
790 N. Woodward
Birmingham, MI 48011
810 644-2493
Closed weekends.
East side of street in one story retail strip; just north of
Vinewood.

47 Weiss Antique Gallery
800 North Woodward
Birmingham, MI 48011
810 646-2840
North end of retail strip.

48 Azar's Gallery Of Oriental Rugs
670 South Woodward
Birmingham, MI 48011
810 644-7311; 800 622-RUGS
Thurs. to Sat. 10 to 9, Sun. 12 to 5
4 blocks south of Maple, west side of street. Also a
branch in the Merrilwood Building.

49 The Paper Trail
725 South Adams
Birmingham, MI 48009
810 540-2966
Wed. to Sat. 1:30 to 5:30
In the South Adams Square Building, east side of street.
Ephemera & small collectibles.

50 James Sanders, Antiquarian
725 South Adams, South Adams Square Building
Birmingham, MI 48009
810 540-0044
Tues. to Fri. 11 to 4, Sat. 11 to 3

51 Estate Buyers
725 South Adams, South Adams Square Building
Birmingham, MI 48009
810 644-2556
Mon. to Sat. 10 to 5:30
Opened 1994.

52 The Cowboy Trader Gallery
725 South Adams, South Adams Square Building
Birmingham, MI 48009
810 647-8833
Tues. to Sat. 11 to 6
Small shop; western art and antiques.

TROY

53 Judy Frankel & Associates
2900 West Maple Road, Suite 111
Troy , MI 48040
810 649-4399
Mon. to Wed. 10 to 4, Thurs. 10 to 12, or by
appointment.
Lower level of Somerset Plaza office building, next to
Somerset Plaza, northeast corner Maple & Coolidge.
Antiques and decorative arts.

54 Troy Corners Antiques
90 East Square Lake Road
Troy, MI 48098
810 879-9848
Mon. to Sat. 10 to 5
I-75 to Exit 72, Crooks Road north to Square Lake Road
east 1 mile, past Livernois Road, south side of street.
In an 1840 Church. 14 dealers; opened 1964.

BLOOMFIELD HILLS

55 Century Jewelers, Inc.
1591 Opdyke
Bloomfield Hills, MI 48013
810 335-5828
Mon. to Sat. 10:30 to 6
In Bloomfield Hills Shopping Center, Square Lake Road.
Diamonds, Coins & Antiques.

ROCHESTER

56 Antiques by Pamela
331 Main Street
Rochester, MI 48063
810 652-0866
Mon. to Wed. & Fri. 10 to 6,
Thurs. 10 to 8, Sat. 10 to 5
Downtown, west side of street.
Use Main Street or back parking lot entrances.

57 Haig Galleries
311 Main Street, Floor Two
Rochester, MI 48063
810 656-8333
By appointment.
Downtown, west side of street.
Ancient, Asian, Tribal art.

58 Sally Sewer Antiques
305 Main Street
Rochester, MI 48063
810 540-9415
Seldom open.
West side of street, above Alvins clothing store.

59 Haig Jewelers
436 South Main
Rochester, MI 48063
810 652-3660
Mon. to Sat. 10 to 6; open to 9 Thurs. & Fri.
Downtown, east side of street.
Antique jewelry.

60 Mahogany on Main
404 Main Street
Rochester, MI 48063
810 652-6860
Mon. to Sat. 11 to 5, Sun. by chance.
Downtown, east side of street.
Mahogany furniture, etc.

PONTIAC

61 Antique Mall in Downtown Pontiac
25 North Saginaw Street
Pontiac, MI
810 338-6889
Tues. to Fri. 12:30 to 4
Downtown, west side of street between Pike and
Lawrence.   Beautiful old retail shop interior.

LAKE ORION

62 Elegant Eras
197 South Broadway
Lake Orion, MI 48035
810 693-0303
Thurs. to Sun. 10 to 5
Broadway veers off M-24 to the east just south of
downtown; shop faces M-24, east side of the street.

FARMINGTON HILLS

63 Rosebud
21117 Randall
Farmington Hills, MI 48336
810 684-2668
Mon. to Fri. 9 to 6, Sat. & Sun. by appointment.
North of 8 Mile Road, 1 block east of Merriman Road.

FRANKLIN

64 D & J Bittker, Ltd.
26111 W 14 Mile Road, Suite 102
Franklin, MI 48025
810 932-2660   By Appointment Only
Antique & new Chinese furniture, screens, textiles, etc.

65 Antique Gallery Of Franklin Village
32800 Franklin Road
Franklin Village, MI 48025
810 539-0963
Wed. to Sat. 10:30 to 5:30
South of 14 Mile Road, east side of street, 2nd floor.

Detail Map: South Central Oakland County

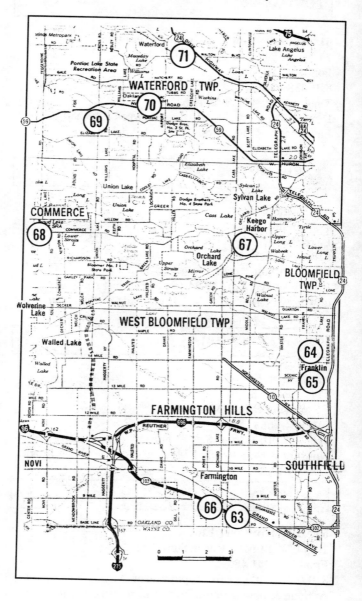

FARMINGTON

66 Hickory Hill Antiques
32315 Grand River Avenue
Farmington, MI 48336
810 477-6630
Daily 10 to 6; Thurs. & Fri. till 8
South side of highway, half mile east of Farmington
Road. Enter the parking lot from the east side of the
building via Brookdale Street, and enter from the rear.
80 dealers. Large high quality mall.

KEEGO HARBOR

67 Matsel's Galleries Inc.
3371 Orchard Lake Road
Keego Harbor, MI 48023
810 682-8270
Tues. to Sat. 11 to 5:30
Corner Orchard Lake Road & Commerce Road,
southeast side of the street.
Reproductions and antiques.

COMMERCE

68 Byers Country Store
213 Commerce Road
Commerce, MI 48382
810 363-3638
Wed. to Sun. 11:30 to 5
South side of highway, just west of Carol Lake Road.
Antiques, collectibles, country store items; farm house
in back with furniture.

WHITE LAKE

69 Moon Valley House Antiques & Uniques
8355 Highland Road
White Lake, MI 48095
810 666-1500
Mon. to Sat. 10 to 5, Sun. 12 to 4; closed Sundays June
to August.
South side of highway, west of Williams Lake Road.
Country, primitives, folk art, decorating services.

WATERFORD

70 Shop Of Antiquity
7766 Highland (M-59)
Waterford, MI 48329
810 666-2333
Tues. to Sun. 11 to 5
North side of highway, east of Williams Lake Road.
Country furniture, old fork art, hooked rugs.

71 The Great Midwestern Antique Emporium
5233 Dixie Highway (U.S. 24)
Waterford, MI 48329
810 623-7460
Tues. to Sun. 10 to 5
West side of highway, 6 blocks south of Andersonville
Road.
50 dealers, 5,500 square feet

CLARKSTON

72 Calcote Country
South Main Street
Clarkston, MI 48346
810 625-7440
Mon. to Fri. 11 to 5, Sat. 10 to 6
Downtown, west side of street, half block south of light.

73 Creation's Best
50 South Main Street
Clarkston, MI 48346
810 625-4340
Mon. to Fri. 9 to 6, Sat. 9 to 5
House on a hill, 1 block south of the downtown light,
west side of street. If approaching from the south: just
after the Waldon Street light is a church with white
steeple; the shop is just north of that and the entrance to
the parking lot is on the north side of the shop.
Flowers, gifts, and antiques.

Creations Best
in
The Parsonage

Shirley Wilson, *owner*
810 / 625-4340

50 South Main Street
Clarkston, MI 48346
1-800 / 322-0922

74 Pour Mary's Antiques & Things
2 East Washington Street
Clarkston , MI 48346
810 625-6716
Tues. to Sat. 10 to 5, Sun. 11 to 3
Downtown, north side of street, just east of the light.
Antiques and collectibles.

75 Daisy Dowling Antiques
21 North Main
Clarkston, MI 48346
810 625-3122
Mon. to Sat. 10:30 to 5, Sun. by appointment.
Downtown, west side of street, just north of light.

76 Beverly's Flowers, Gifts & Antiques
7150 North Main (M-15) (Note: there is no relationship
between the street numbering system in Village and the
Township of Clarkston. This shop is only a few blocks
north of downtown.)
Clarkston, MI 48346
810 625-5020
Mon. to Sat. 10 to 6, Sun. by chance;
Nov. & Dec. Sun. 11 to 4
1 block south of I-75, east side of street.
Flowers, gifts, some antiques used as gift display props.

SOUTH LYON

77 Parkway Antiques
112 East Lake
South Lyon, MI 48178
810 437-2840
Mon. to Sat. 10 to 4
Small shop in back of South Lyon Pharmacy, Southeast
Corner East Lake (10 Mile Road) and Lafayette, at the
light. Collectibles, used furniture, some antiques.

78 Pegasus Antiques & Collectibles
105 North Lafayette
South Lyon, MI 48178
810 437-0320
May to Sept.: Daily 11 to 5;
Oct. to Apr.: Tues. to Sun. 11 to 5
Downtown, west side of street, north of 10 Mile Road.

Detail Map: South Lyon

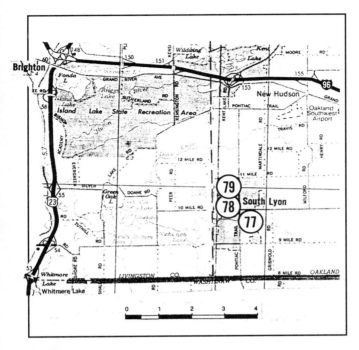

79 Cabbage Rose Ltd.
317 North Lafayette
South Lyon, MI 48178
810 486-0930
Tues. to Sat. 10 to 5, Sun. 12 to 5
Pink house, north of downtown, west side of street.
Returning to I-96 go north on Lafayette Street (Pontiac
Trail) to the end at a "T" intersection 2 miles north of
town; the sign says I-96 is to the right, but to reach the
nearest exit go left (west) 1/4 mile to Kent Lake Road,
then north 1 mile to I-96.

DAVISBURG

80 Marie Vermilye Antiques & Collectibles
12461 Scott Road
Davisburg, MI 48350
810 634-9052
April to Oct.: Sat. 9:30 to 5, Sun. 10 to 5
South from Davisburg on Andersonville Road to Hall
Road, South on Hall to Scott.

HOLLY

81 Balcony Row Antiques
216 South Broad Street
Holly, MI 48442
810 634-1400
Thurs. to Sat. 10:30 to 5, Sun. 1 to 5
West side of the street.

82 Water Tower Antiques Mall
310 South Broad
Holly, MI 48442
810 634-3500
Mon. to Sat. 10 to 5; Sun. 12 to 5
Downtown, across from the Water Tower.
60 dealers

83 Holly Crossing Antiques
219 South Broad
Holly, MI 48442
810 634-3333
Fri. & Sat. 11 to 5, Sun. 12 to 5
East side of the street.

84 Battle Alley Arcade
108 Battle Alley
Holly , MI 48442
810 634-8800
Mon. to Sat. 10:30 to 5:30; Sun. 12 to 5:30
Downtown, between Broad & Saginaw Streets, next to
the Holly Hotel.
25 craft and antique booths.

85 Your Heart's Memories
2280 Fenton Road (also called Holly Road)
Holly, MI 48442
810 634-9879
Summer only.
South from Holly on Broad Street which becomes
Medford Road; at the "T" intersection a mile south of
town go west on Fenton (aka Holly) Road. Shop is in
shed next to house on south side of road 0.6 mile west
of Fish Lake Road. Look for the chain link fence.

3.3 LIVINGSTON COUNTY

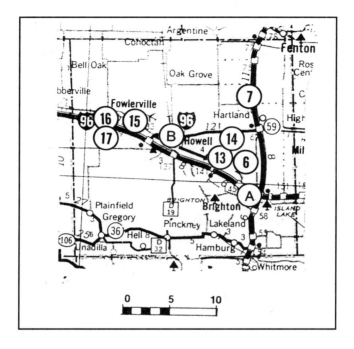

A. Brighton: 1 to 5 (See Detail Map)
B. Howell: 8 to 14

Recommended Points of Interest:
1. Brighton: Summer Folk Art Festival at Mill Pond.

Additional Information:
Brighton Area Chamber of Commerce, 810 227-5086

BRIGHTON

1 Mill Pond Antique Galleries
217 West Main Street
Brighton, MI 48116
810 229-8686
Mon. to Wed. 10 to 7, Thurs. 10 to 8, Fri. 10 to 9,
Sat. 10 to 5, Sun. 12 to 5
Downtown, 1 block west of Grand River Road, south.
Jewelry, antiques, and vintage watches.

2 Entre' Nous Antiques and Accessories
323 West Main Street
Brighton, MI 48116
810 229-8686
Tues. to Fri. 11 to 5, Sat. 10:30 to 4:30
2 blocks west of Grand River Road, down a walk-way.

3 Brighton Antiques & Crafts Mall
409 West Main Street
Brighton, MI 48116
810 229-0778
Mon. to Sat. 10 to 6, Sun. 12 to 5
West of downtown, south side of street.

4 Quaker Shoppe Antiques
210 Hyne Street
Brighton, IN 48116
810 231-3530; 810 229-6558
Thurs. to Sat. 11 to 4, or by appointment.
1 block south of West Main Street, west side of street.

5 Nostalgia
416 West Main Street
Brighton, MI 48116
810 229-4710
Mon. to Fri. 10 to 7, Sat. 10 to 5, Sun. 12 to 5;
(Open 9 a.m. Sat. during the summer.)
West of downtown, north side of street.
Antiques, advertising, Coca Cola, Juke Boxes, vintage
clothing, primitives, toys, glassware, etc.

Detail Map: Brighton

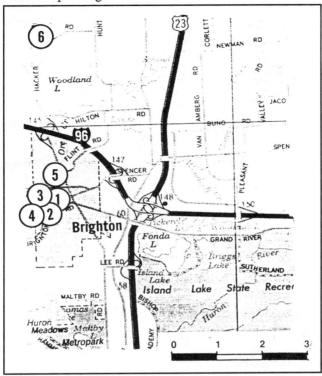

6 Stock Exchange Antique Shop
1156 Hacker Road
Brighton, MI 48116
313 227-7912
Apr. to Jan.: Daily 12 to 6
West on Grand River Road 1 mile to Hacker Road;
north on Hacker 1.5 miles; east side of road.

Stock Exchange
Antique Shop
1156 Hacker Rd.
Brighton, Michigan
(313) 227-7912
Specialized in Country Furniture

HARTLAND

7 The Shenandoah Shoppe
3568 Avon
Hartland, MI 48029
810 632-5560
Mon. to Sat. 11 to 5; Sun. 12 to 4
From U.S. 23 go east on M-59 to light at frontage road,
then north 1 1/4 mile.   Country gifts and antiques.

HOWELL

8 Ray Egnash Antiques and Auctions
202 South Michigan Ave.
Howell, MI 48843
517 546-2005
Tues. to Sat. 10 to 5
West side of street, 1 block south of downtown light.

9 W. D. Adams Antique Mall
201 East Grand River Avenue
Howell, MI 48843
517 546-5360
Mon. to Sat. 10 to 6; Sun. 11 to 5
Across from courthouse.
40 dealers

10 Victorian Gardens
128 East Sibley
Howell, MI 48843
517 546-6749
Tues. to Sat. 10 to 6; Nov. 28 to Dec. 24 open 7 days.
One block south of Grand River Avenue, in back of
Adams Antiques.
Antiques, gifts, garden shop.

11 My Girls Treasures
2651 East Grand River Avenue
Howell, MI 48843
517 548-3808
Every day 12 to 6
1.5 miles east of downtown light, north side of highway.

12 Yesterday's Treasures
2649 East Grand River Avenue
Howell, MI 48843
517 546-8385
Every day 12 to 6
East of downtown, north side of highway.

13 Lake Chemung Oldies
5255 East Grand River Avenue
Howell, MI 48843
517 546-8875
Wed. to Sat. by appointment.
North side of highway, five miles east of Howell.

14 Touch of Country
5640 East Highland (M-59)
Howell, MI 48843
517 546-5995
Mon. to Sat. 10 to 6, Thurs. until 8
3 miles east of Howell, south side of street.
Gifts, crafts, reproductions, nostalgia, collectibles.

FOWLERVILLE

15 Lone Pine Antique Furniture
4141 East Grand River Road
Fowlerville, MI 48836
517 546-6780
Usually open; shop in home.
South side of highway.
Building for sale, and shop very likely to close in 1994.

16 Ruth's Resale Shop
102 East Grand River Road
Fowlerville, MI 48836
517 223-7221
By chance.
Downtown, southwest corner at stop light.

17 S & J Track Shack
514 South Grand Avenue
Fowlerville, MI 48836
517 223-7442
Tues. to Sat. 10 to 5
I-96 Exit 129 north; west side of street at the tracks.

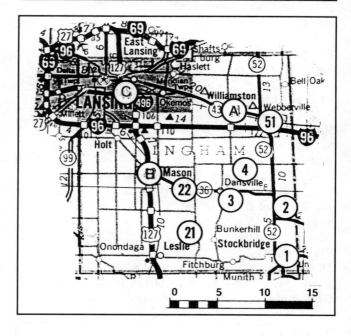

A. Williamston: 5 to 20
B. Mason: 23 to 31
C. Lansing Area: 32 to 50 (See Detail Map)

Recommended Points of Interest:
1. Lansing: State Capitol, 517 335-1483
2. Lansing: Michigan Historical Museum, 717 West Allegan.
3. Lansing: City Market, Cedar & Shiawassee. 517 483-4300
4. East Lansing: Beal Botanical Garden, West Circle Drive
between Main Library & Sports Building. 517 355-9582
Additional Information:
Lansing Convention & Visitors Bureau, 517 487-6800

STOCKBRIDGE

1 Tom Forshee Antiques
119 West Main Street P.O. Box 125
Stockbridge, MI 49285
517 851-8114
Fri. & Sat. 10 to 4; Sun. 12 to 4; or by appointment.
South side of street, at the red awning. Entrance from
the rear parking lot. Oriental & English porcelains;
American furniture

2   White Oak Antiques
4665 East Cooper Road
Stockbridge, MI 49285
517 851-8151
By chance.
7 miles north of Stockbridge on M-52 (or 8 miles south
of I-96), and one-half mile east of M-52.
Antiques and collectible junk.

DANSVILLE

3   Red Barn Antiques & Collectibles
1131 Mason Street (M-36)
Dansville, MI 48819
517 623-6631
May 1 to Nov. 1: Fri. to Sun. 11 to 5
West edge of town, north side of street.

WILLIAMSTON

4   Bittersweet Antiques
2200 Howell Road
Williamston, MI 48895
517 655-1698
By chance or appointment.
South 6 miles on Williamston to T intersection with
Howell Road; turn east; 3rd house on south side of road.
Country, quilts, depression glass, etc.

5   Gray Goose Antiques
150 South Putnam Street
Williamston, MI 48895
517 655-4043
Mon. to Sat. 10 to 5; Sun. by appointment.
Downtown, west side of street.
6 dealers; coop shop.

6   Lyon's Den Antiques
132 South Putnam Street
Williamston, MI 48895
517 655-2622
Wed. to Sat. 1 to 5, Sun. 12 to 5
Mon. & Tues. 11 to 5 by chance.

7 Putnam Street Antiques
122 South Putnam Street, 2nd floor
Williamston, MI 48895
517 655-4521
Mon. to Sat 10:30 to 5; Sun. 12 to 4
Downtown, west side of street.   16 dealers.

8 The Jolly Coachman
138 East Grand River Avenue
Williamston, MI 48895
517 655-6606
Wed. to Sun. 10 to 5
Downtown, south side of street.   7 dealers.

9 Happicats Antiques
133 East Grand River Avenue
Williamston, MI 48895
517 655-1251; 517 223-8039
By chance; seldom open.
Downtown, north side of street.
Cat collectibles, vintage clothing, etc.

10 Pieces of the Past
127 East Grand River
Williamston, MI 48895
517 655-3653
Tues. to Sun. 11 to 5
Downtown, north side of street.

11 Old Village Antiques
125 East Grand River Avenue
Williamston, MI 48895
517 655-4827
April thru Dec.: Tues. to Sat. 10 to 5, Sun. 12 to 5;
Jan. thru March: Fri. & Sat. 10 to 5, Sun. 12 to 5
Downtown, north side of street, east of light.
Wallace Nutting prints; walnut & cherry victorian
furniture, art, glass, etc.

12 Beer & Things
100 East Grand River Avenue
Williamston, MI 48895
517 655-6701
Tues. to Fri. 12 to 7, Sat. 10 to 5
Downtown.
Beer collectibles; new & antique brewing equipment.

13 Corner Cottage
120 High Street
Williamston, MI 48895
517 655-3257
Wed. to Sat. 11 to 5
Downtown, just east of Putnam.
Refinished oak furniture, etc.

14 Legends Jewelry
104 West Grand River Avenue
Williamston, MI 48895
517 655-4221
Mon. to Sat. 10 to 5
Downtown
Estate jewelry.

15 Main Street Shoppe Antiques
108 West Grand River Avenue,   Downtown
Williamston, MI 48895
517 655-4005
Mon. to Sat. 10:30 to 5; Sun. 12 to 5
10 dealers.

16 Consignments of Williamston
115 West Grand River Avenue,   Downtown
Williamston, MI 48895
517 655-6064
Mon. to Sat. 10 to 6, Sun. 12 to 6
Antiques, collectibles, used things.

17 Old Plank Road Antiques
126 West Grand River Avenue
Williamston, MI 48895
517 655-4273
Summer: Tues. to Sat. 10 to 5; Winter: Tues. to Sat.
11 to 5
Downtown, north side of street.

18 The Vintage Years
540 West Grand River Avenue
Williamston, MI 48895
517 655-1340
Mon. to Sat. 10:30 to 5:30; Sun. 12 to 5:30
Northeast corner Grand River Avenue & McCormick,
several blocks west of downtown.
Books, dried flowers, antiques.

19 Poor Richard's Antiques
834 West Grand River Avenue
Williamston, MI 48895
517 655-2455
Wed. to Sat. 12 to 5
Northeast corner West Grand Avenue & Wint Street,
eight blocks west of downtown.
Costume jewelry, etc.

20 Grand River Merchants Antique Market
1039 West Grand River
Williamston, MI 48895
517 655-1350
Mon. to Sat. 10 to 5; Sun. 12 to 5:30
1 mile west of downtown stop light.
70 dealers, 15,000 square feet.
Opened 1981.

LESLIE

21 Anns'tiques
4202 Meridian Road
Leslie, MI 49251
517 589-9225
March to Dec.: Wed., Fri. & Sat. 12 to 5
West side of road between Kinneville and Fitchburg
Roads. 4 1/2 miles east of U.S. 127.

MASON

22 Sally's Unique Jewelry & Antiques
652 West Dexter Trail
Mason, MI 48854
517 676-1786
By chance.
2 1/2 miles southeast of Kipp Road, north side of road.
Barn in back of house. (Formerly Lil & Sal's Antiques)

23   Mason Antiques Market
Mason Street
Mason, MI 48854
517 676-9753; 517 676-1270
Every day 10 to 6
Mason Antiques District

24   The Garment District
Mason Street
Mason, MI 48854
517 676-9753
7 Days 10 to 6
Mason Antiques District; upstairs from Mason Antique
Market.
Vintage apparel.

25   The Carriage Shop
Mason Street
Mason, MI 48854
517 676-1530
Wed. to Sun. 10 to 6
Mason Antique District, in back of the Mason Antiques
Market.
Toys, Dolls, Disney, Jewelry

26   Chapman's Old Mill Antiques Mall
207 Mason Street
Mason, MI 48854
517 676-1270
Every day 10 to 5
Mason Antique District

27   Front Porch Antiques
Mason Street
Mason, MI 48854
517 676-6388
Every day 10 to 6
Mason Antique District

28   The Loft Antiques Co-Op
Mason Street
Mason, MI 48854
517 676-0400
Wed. to Sun. 10 to 6
Mason Antique District, upstairs from The Front Porch.

29   Peddlers Row
Mason Street
Mason, MI 48854
No telephone.
Summer only: Every day 10 to 6
Mason Antique District
Outdoor sheds.

30   The Country House
Mason Street: Mason Antique District
Mason, MI 48854
517 676-1045
Wed. to Sun. 10 to 6

31   Rusty Nail Warehouse
Mason Street
Mason, MI 48854
Every day 10 to 6
Mason Antique District

OKEMOS

32   Farm Village Antique Mall
3448 Hagadorn Road
Okemos , MI 48864
517 337-3266;   517 337-4988
Mon. to Sat. 11 to 6, Thurs. to 8; Sun 12 to 6
Southeast corner Hagadorn & Jolly Streets.
Large multi-level facility, 35 dealers, 25,000 sq. ft.

33   Spud's Shop
3448 Hagadorn Road
Okemos, MI 48864
517 351-2140
Summer: Sat. & Sun. 1 to 5
Just outside Farm Village Antique Mall.

34   Wooden Skate Antiques
1259 W Grand River
Okemos , MI 48864
517 349-1515; FAX 517 349-8628
Mon. to Sat. 10 to 5:30, Thurs. to 8
Southeast corner Cornell Road & Grand River, 1.3 miles
east of Meridian Mall, 6 miles west of Williamston.
Estate jewelry, glass, china, furniture, etc.

35   Sentimental Journey Antiques
1259 West Grand River
Okemos, MI 48864
517 349-1515
Mon. to Sat. 10 to 5:30, Thurs. to 8.
Upstairs in Wooden Skate Antiques.
Collective group of dealers; opened 1993.

Detail Map: Lansing

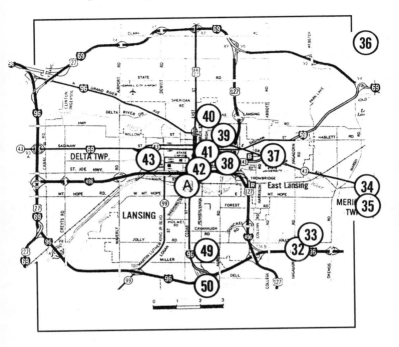

EAST LANSING

36 Wooden Shoe Antique House
14944 Upton Road
East Lansing , MI 48823
517 641-6040
Mon. to Sat. 9 to 6; Sun. 1:30 to 5; or by appointment
to 9 p.m.
North of I-69; 1.5 miles north of Old M-78, west side of
Upton. Actually in Clinton County, but with an East
Lansing (Ingham County) address.
Glass, china, primitives, old furniture.

37 Prints Ancient & Modern
515 East Grand River Avenue
East Lansing, MI 48823
517 337-6366
Mon. to Wed. 10 to 6, Thurs. & Fri. 10 to 9,
Sat. 10 to 5
Second floor.

LANSING

38 Slightly Tarnished
2008 East Michigan
Lansing, MI 48912
517 485-3599
Mon. to Sat. 11 to 5:30
1/4 block west of Clemens Street, south side of street.
Used items, some antiques.

39 Classic Arms Company
1600 Lake Lansing Road
Lansing , MI 48912
517 484-6112
Mon. to Fri. 9 to 6, Sat. 9 to 5
One mile west of U.S. 127, south side of street.
Antique guns.

40 Eberly's Emporium
3200 North East Street
Lansing , MI 48912
517 484-3355
Open by chance.
Northeast corner East Street & Community Street.

41 Bob's Antiques
617 East Michigan
Lansing, MI
517 485-2177
Fri. & Sat. 10 to 4 by chance.
North side of street.
Small shop.

42   Triola's
119 Pere Marquette
Lansing , MI 48912
517 484-5414
Mon. to Fri. 12 to 5, or by appointment.
1 block east of Larch, 1 block south of Shiawassee, in
loft district just east of downtown.
Deco and modernism design.

43   Bohnet's
1712 W. Saginaw Street (East-bound N-43)
Lansing , MI 48915
517 482-2654
Mon. to Fri. 8 to 5; also Sat. in winter.
Light fixtures.

44   Rebecca's Antiques
1101 South Washington
Lansing , MI 48910
517 485-6076
Mon. to Sat. 11 to 5
Southeast corner Washington & Elm Streets.

45 Gallimores
1113 South Washington
Lansing, MI 48910
517 485-9843
Wed. to Sat. 11 to 5
East side of street.
Opened 1994. Antiques, collectibles, and reproductions.

46 Somebody Else's Stuff
1137 South Washington
Lansing, MI 48910
517 482-8886
Mon. to Fri. 11 to 6; Sat. 12 to 5
East side of the street.

47 River Front Emporium
1100 block South Washington
Lansing, MI 48910
No telephone listed at press time.
Days & hours not available at press time.
West side of street.
Proposed to open 1994.

48 Stark Raving Neon
1147 South Washington
Lansing , MI 48910
517 487-1310
By chance or appointment.
East side of the street.
Neon signs and art.

49 Antique Connection
5411 South Cedar St.
Lansing , MI 48911
517 882-8700
Mon. to Fri. 10 to 9; Sat. 10 to 6; Sun. 12 to 5
East side of street, in back of Furniture Connection
furniture store, 1 mile north of I-96, 1 block south of
Jolly Road.
Crafts, glass, smalls, with some antique furniture used
as accents in the furniture store. 90 antique & crafts
booths.

HOLT

50 Antiques Plus
Cedar Park Shopping Center, 2495 N. Cedar
Holt, MI 48842
517 694-5767
Mon. to Fri. 11 to 6, Sat. 10 to 5, Sun. 12 to 5, Thurs.
to 9
West side of highway, just south of I-96.
The mall was expanded in 1993.

WEBBERVILLE

51 Re-Use It Antiques, Consignments & Collectibles
120 West Grand River
Webberville MI 48892
517 521-4390
Tues. to Sun. 10:30 to 5:30
Downtown, south side of the street.
5 miles east of Williamston, 11 miles west of Howell.
General line of furniture.

TIER 4:
THE I-69 ROUTE

4.1 ST. CLAIR COUNTY

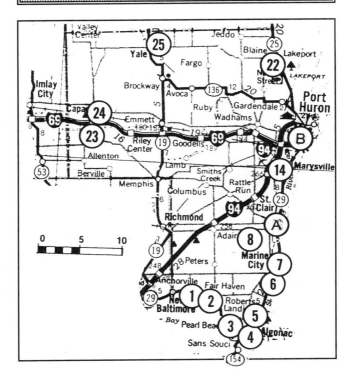

A. St. Clair: 9 to 13
B. Port Huron: 15 to 21 (See Detail Map)

Recommended Points of Interest:
1. Port Huron: Museum of Arts and History, 1115 6th Street.
Additional Information:
Blue Water Convention & Tourism Bureau, 800 852-4242

ANCHORVILLE

1 Hideaway
9860 Dixie Highway (M-29)
Anchorville, MI 48004
810 725-3843
Wed. to Sun 11 to 5
House on north side of street, west of post office.

FAIR HAVEN

2 The Cooperage
8832 Dixie
Fair Haven, MI 48023
810 725-2484
Mon. to Fri. 12 to 4 and 5:30 to 7:30; Sat. 10 to 5
North side of road, east of Ira Road.
Military items, watches, crafts.

ALGONAC

3 Early Attic Antiques
5216 Pointe Tremble
Algonac, MI 48001
810 794-7117, or 800 690-LAMP
Daily 11 to 5; Closed Tues.
2 1/2 mi. West of Algonac; 1/2 block east of Ainsworth
Street, north side of highway.

4 Remember When
2210 St. Clair River
Algonac, MI 48001
810 794-1050
Thurs. to Sun. 11 to 5
North of downtown, east side of street. Glassware, etc.

5 The Snuggery
8540 North River Road (MI Route 29)
Algonac, MI 48001
810 765-4737
Mar. 15 to Jan. 15: Tues. to Sun. 12 to 5;
Jan. 15 to Mar. 15: Fri. to Sun. 10 to 6
Just north of Algonac State Park, west side of highway.

MARINE CITY

6 Marine City Antique Warehouse
105 Fairbanks
Marine City, MI 48039
810 765-1119
Every Day 10 to 5
In Bell River Plaza; entrance on west side of building.

7 Shipmaster's General Store
204 South Water Street
Marine City, MI 48039
810 765-2975
Tues. to Sat. 10 to 5:30; Sun. 11 to 4
Southwest corner Jefferson & South Water.

CHINA

8 Red Barn Antiques
4950 King Road
China, MI 48054
810 765-9453
Fri. 3 to 7, Sat. 10 to 5, Sun. 11 to 6, Mon. 10 to 6
King Road is a mile west of downtown Marine City;
north on King Road to just past Meisner Road; west side
of road.

ST. CLAIR

9 John Moffett Antiques
1102 South 7th St.
St. Clair, MI 48079
810 329-3300
Wed. to Sun 12 to 5 by appointment.
1/2 block north of F.W. Moore Highway; red brick
building.

10 Antique Inn
302 Thornapple
St. Clair, MI 48079
810 329-5833
Tues. to Sat. 11 to 5
Purple house, northwest corner 3rd & Thornapple
Streets.

11 Wallpaper World
201 North Riverside
Riverview Plaza Shopping Center
St. Clair, MI 48079
810 329-9110
Mon. to Sat. 9:30 to 5; Fri. to 6
Do not be misled by its name; it is a fine antique shop.

RIVERTOWN ANTIQUES

FEATURING THE UNIQUE & UNUSUAL

MILITARIA - AMERICANA - PAINTINGS

ROGER REYNOLDS
201 N. Riverside Ave.   **810 329-1020**
St. Clair, MI 48070

Riverview Plaza

12 Rivertown Antiques
201 North Riverside
Riverview Plaza Shopping Center
St. Clair , MI 48079
810 329-1020
Thurs. to Mon. 10 to 4
South end of mall, facing the River.
Small shop; art & Americana.

13 Jennifer's Trunk
Riverview Plaza Shopping Center
201 North Riverside
St. Clair, MI 48079
810 329-2032
Wed. to Sat. 12 to 5, Sun. 12 to 3:30
Art and folk art.

MARYSVILLE

14 Old Times 'N' Such
1305 Gratiet
Marysville, MI 48040
810 364-3650
Thurs. to Sat. 12 to 5
2 blocks north of Michigan Avenue, southeast side of
street.
Glassware, etc.

Detail Map: Port Huron

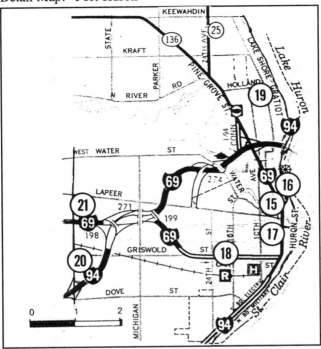

To get downtown: From I-94 take Business Loop 69
which becomes Griswold Street to the end at Military;
go left on Military, which becomes Huron Avenue.

PORT HURON

15 Rick Currie & Son, Goldsmiths,
Don Butkovich Antiques
506 Grand River Avenue
Port Huron, MI 48060
810 982-7269
Mon. to Sat. 10 to 5:30, Fri. to 8
Downtown, south side of street, just west of Huron Av.

16 Citadel Gallery
609 Huron Avenue
Port Huron
MI 48060, John & Janice Meinhardt
Mon. to Sat. 11 to 5; Usually: the 2nd Weekend of the
month 11 to end of auction.
Downtown, northwest corner Bard & Huron.

17 The Used Furniture Outlet
1219 Military Street
Port Huron, MI 48060
810 987-4001
Mon. to Sat. 10 to 5:30
West side of street between Court and Union.
Used furniture, some antiques.

18 Antique Collectors Corner
1603 Griswold Street
Port Huron, MI 48060
Store: 810 982-2780; Home: 810 984-2932
Thurs. to Sat. 12 to 5
Northwest corner 16th Street & Griswold, southwest
side of city. Small crowded shop in former gas station.

19 Under the Bridge
2333 Gratiot
Port Huron, MI 48060
810 982-4063
By chance.
From downtown: North on Pine Grove (i.e. Business
Route I-94) to Stone Street; north on Stone 7 blocks to
State Street; east 5 blocks to Gratiot, then north.

20 The Tulip Tree
1428 North Range Road
Port Huron, MI 48060
810 364-9077
Fri. & Sat. 12 to 5
Just west of I-94 at Exit 269.
Antiques and collectibles.

21 Yesterday's Treasures
4490 Lapeer Road West
Port Huron, MI 48060
810 982-2100
Tues. to Fri. 10 to 6; Sat. 10 to 5
Southeast corner Range Road & Lapeer Road West.
Antiques, coins, stamps, gifts, collectibles.

LAKEPORT

22 Antique Workshop
7077 Lakeshore (M-25)
Lakeport, MI 48059
810 385-4344
Tues. to Fri. 10 to 6
6 miles North of Port Huron.

CAPAC

23 Yesterday's Shadows
127 North Main Street (Capac Road)
Capac, MI 48014
810 395-4100
Tue. & Thurs. 12 to 5; Wed. & Fri. 10 to 7; Sat. 10 to
3, Sun. 12 to 4
Downtown, west side of street.
Antiques, crafts, and collectibles.

24 Town Crier
5214 Capac Road
Capac, MI 48014
810 395-7230
By appointment only.
1 1/2 miles north of town, east side of road.

YALE

25 Yale Antiques Mall
110 South Main Street
Yale, MI 48097
810 387-2261
Scheduled to be open every day.
10 miles north of I-69 on M-19
Proposed at press time for a 1994 opening.

4.2 LAPEER COUNTY

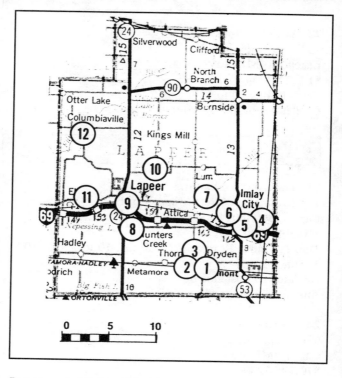

Recommended Points of Interest:
1. Lapeer: County Court House, 148 West Nepessing Street;
1845 Greek revival.

DRYDEN

1 A Basket of Violets
5508 Main
Dryden, MI 48428
810 796-3244
Mon. to Sat. to 5
Downtown, south side of street, just east of light.
Flowers, gifts, some antiques.

2 Time Gazer Antiques & Collectibles
5489 Main
Dryden, MI 48428
810 796-2960
Tues. to Sat. 12 to 5, Thurs. to 6
Downtown, north side of street, just west of stop light.

3 Remember When
3960 North Mill Road
Dryden, MI 48428
810 796-2889
Tues. to Sun. 12 to 5, Fri. to 9
West side of street, half block north of light.
Multi-dealer shop opened 1994.

IMLAY CITY

4 Re-Sale Shop
7567 Imlay City Road (Old M-21)
Imlay City, MI 48444
810 724-1082
Mon. to Sat. 10 to 6; Sun. 12:30 to 5:30
1 1/2 miles east of M-53.
Collectibles, used stuff, etc.

5 Victorian House Antiques
240 North Main Street
Imlay City, MI 48444
810 724-9245
By appointment only.
Large Victorian house on the east side of street, north of
downtown. No sign.

6 Memory Junction
244 East 3rd Street
Imlay City, MI 48444
810 724-4811
Mon. to Sat. 10 to 5
Downtown, southwest corner Main & 3rd Streets.

7 The Bayberry House
426 North Summers Road
Imlay City, MI 48444
810 724-6307
By chance or appointment.
From Imlay City: West several miles on M-21 to
Summers, then south; east side of the road.

LAPEER

8 Lapeer House of Antiques
1733 S. Lapeer Road (M-24)
Lapeer, MI 48446
810 667-9476
By appointment only.
East side of street, one half mile south of I-69 at Lake
Forest Drive.

9 Twice Is Nice Classics, Inc.
477 West Nepessing
Lapeer, MI 48446
810 664-8463
Mon. to Fri. 10 to 5; Sat. 10 to 4
West end of downtown, south side of street.

10 Past Tense Antiques
1965 Farnsworth
Lapeer , MI 48446
810 664-5559
Mon. to Sat. 10 to 6; Sun. 12-6
M-24 3 miles north to Daley Road, turn right to
Farnsworth, turn right.

11 Windy Knoll Antiques & Collectibles
5297 West Oregon Road
Lapeer, MI 48446
810 664-4009
By chance or appointment.
South side of road, 5 miles west of Lapeer, just west of
Maple Leaf Road.
Specializing in Tea Leaf, Ironstone, & Depression
Glass.

COLUMBIAVILLE

12 Christina's Antiques & Things
5155 Stanley Road
Columbiaville, MI 48421
810 793-2762
Usually Mon. to Sat. 10 to 6; call ahead in winter.
4 miles east of M-15.

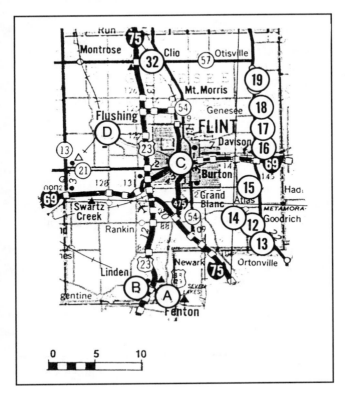

A. Fenton: 1 to 3
B. Linden: 4 to 11
C. Flint: 20 to 26 (See Detail Map)
D. Flushing: 27 to 31

Recommended Points of Interest:
1. Flint: Sloan Museum, 1221 East Kearsley. 313 760-1169
2. Flint: Institute of Arts. 1120 East Kearsley Street.
313 234-1695
3. Flint: Riverbank Park, downtown along the Flint River.
4. Flint: Crossroads Village and Hucklebery Railroad, Bray
Road north of Coldwater Road. Mid-May to Labor Day;
weekends only to Mid-Oct. 1912 carousel, 19th Century
buildings, etc. 313 763-7100
5. Fenton: Tom Walker's Gristmill, 8507 Parshallville Road,
313 629-9079. Also a cider mill and country store. Open
September to mid-November.

Additional Information:
Flint Conv. & Visitors Bureau, 313 232-8900.

FENTON

1 McGehee's Closet
300 South Leroy
Fenton , MI 48430
810 750-8008
Mon. to Sat. 10 to 5
South of the downtown area, west side of street.
Custom made lampshades and supplies.

2 The Gathering
115 Mill
Fenton, MI 48430
810 750-0877
Tues., Wed., Sat. 10 to 5:30; Thurs. & Fri. 12 to 5:30
Southeast corner Mill & Adelaide. Oak & pine furniture.

3 Stuff 'N Such
11440 Torrey Road
Fenton, MI 48430
810 629-4613
Mon. 11 to 7, Tues. to Sat. 9 to 5
West side of road, 1/4 mile south of Thompson Road.

LINDEN

4 The Tangled Vine
131 East Broad Street
Linden, MI 48451
810 735-4611
Tues. to Sat. 10 to 5
Linen, China, wicker, gifts, antiques.

5 Linden Antique Mall
115 E. Broad Street
Linden, MI 48451
810 735-7188
Every day 11 to 6
Downtown, north side of street, 1/2 block east of light.

6 Thimbleberry Antiques
103 West Broad
Linden, MI 48451
810 735-7324
Tues. 11 to 5; Thurs. 11 to 8; Sat. & Sun. by chance or
appointment.
North side of street, 1/4 block west of light.

7 Susan's Woven Seats
116 West Broad Street
Linden, MI 48451
810 735-5854, 810 735-5832
Tues. to Fri. 10 to 4, Sat. 10 to 6
North side of street, 2nd floor above a basket weaving
shop.

8 This & That Shop
418 West Broad Street
Linden, MI 48451
810 735-4234
By chance.
Shed in back of blue house, 3 blocks west of light, north
side of street.

9 Winds of Time Antiques & Furniture Restoration
623 West Broad
Linden, MI 48451
810 735-1104
Hours not available.
West end of town, south side of street, across from
Linden True Value Hardware.
Was in process of preparing to open at press time.

10 Colleen's Collectibles & Antiques
208 North Bridge Street
Linden, MI 48451
810 735-7188
Tues. to Sat. 11 to 5; Sun. & Mon. by chance.
East side of road, 1 block north of light. In the old
firehall on Shiawassee River.
Specializing in oak, wicker, Victorian furniture, china,
glass & quilts.

11 North Side Store Antiques & More
918 Bridge Street
Linden, MI 48451
810 735-4700
Summer: Tues. to Sat. 9 to 6
Winter: By Chance
East side of road just over railroad tracks.

GOODRICH

12 The Flea Market
Eagle Road
Goodrich, MI 48438
No telephone listed.
Open by chance.
East end of downtown, south side of street.

13 Sassafrass Antiques
8082 South State Road (M-15)
Goodrich, MI 48438
810 636-7970
By chance or appointment; please call.
West side of highway 2 houses south of Hegel Road.
Specializing in children's furniture and salesman's
samples.

ATLAS

14 Hear Ye! Hear Ye! Antiques
8530 Perry Road
Atlas, MI 48411
810 636-7163
Summer: Daily except. Mon. & Fri. 1 to 5;
Winter: by appointment.
South side of street.

15 Maurice Reid Antiques
8470 Perry Road PO Box 132
Atlas, MI 48411
810 636-2414
Every Day 10 to 5, closed winter days with bad
weather.

DAVISON

16 Small Town Coins
324 North Main
Davison, MI 48423
810 658-1992
Mon. to Fri. 10 to 5, Sat. 10 to 3
Downtown
Coins, antique toys, etc.

17 Pumpkin Patch Antiques
421 North State Road (M-15)
Davison, MI 48423
810 653-3660
Tues. to Sat. 11 to 5
Shop behind the house.

18 Rayola Flower Shop
919 North State Street (M-15)
Davison, MI 48423
810 653-4177
Mon. to Sat. 8 to 6
North of Davidson Road.
Antiques in room off of flower shop.

19 Cliff's Nostalgia
7050 North State Road (M-15)
Davison, MI 48423
810 658-1126
Fri. 11 to 5; Sat. & Sun. 10 to 6
East side of highway, 4.5 miles north of Davison Road.

FLINT

20 Antiques By Cecilia
G-3106 North Center Road
Flint, MI 48506
810 736-0800
Mon. to Sat. 11-6
Small shop in strip mall east side of Center Road, 1/2
block south of Richfield.

Detail Map: Flint

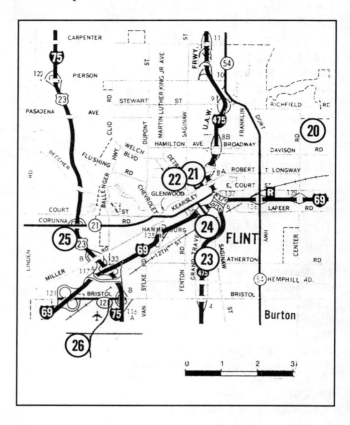

21 Donald J. Schoellig Bookseller
420 East Blvd. Drive
Flint, MI 48503
810 767-7850
Tues., Thurs., Sat. 10 to 5
In the Flint City Farmers Market, 2 blocks west of I-475
Exit 88A.
Used books; some antiques.

22 Farmer's Market Collectibles
Flint City Farmers Market
420 East Boulevard Drive
Flint, MI 48502
810 239-9276
Tues., Thurs. & Sat. 10 to 3:30
Collectibles, some antiques.

23 Reminisce Antique Mall
3514 South Saginaw
Flint, MI 48503
810 767-4152
Daily 9 to 7
West side of the street at Livingston street. From I-75
take Bristol Road Exit, go east 1 mi to Saginaw Street,
north 3 lights (2 miles) to Livingston. From I-69 take
Saginaw Street Exit, south 1 mile to Livingston Street.
Across from Applegate Chevrolet.
60 dealers.

24 Antique Gallery
651 West Twelfth Street
Flint, MI 48503
810 767-8811
Every day 10 to 6
South side of street between Fenton and Grand Traverse.
60 dealers, 12,800 square feet. Enter parking lot, across
the street to the east, from Oak Street. From I-69 exit
at Hammerburo; go south to end at T intersection; go
east past Fenton Street; south side of street.

25 Antiques on Corunna
2031 Lowden Lane
Flint, MI 48532
810 732-5856
Mon., Fri., & Sat 11 to 5; Sun. 12 to 5
1 block west of I-75 Exit 118; in white house 1 block
south of Corunna Road (West M-21). Across from State
Police Post.

26 Rebel's Junque
4442 Torrey Road
Flint, MI 48507
810 238-0882
Daily 8 to 6; Closed Wed. & Sun.
West side of street, 2 blocks north of Maple Street;
South of Bishop Airport.

FLUSHING

27 Antique Center R & J Needful Things
6398 West Pierson Road
Flushing, MI 48443
810 659-2663
Seven Days 10 to 5
North side of street, 2 1/2 miles west of I-75, Exit 122.
100 dealers.

28 Jerry's Meats Market
1537 East Pierson Road
Flushing, MI 48433
810 659-7283
Mon. to Sat. 9 to 6:30
North side of street, east side of town in Country West
Plaza.
Trunks & other antiques.

29 Flushing Antique Emporium
208 East Main
Flushing, MI 48433
810 659-1919
Mon. to Sat. 10:30 to 5:30, Sun. 1 to 5
Downtown, south side of street, west of McKinley
Street.

30 Trudy's Antiques & Dean's Refinishing Service
113 North McKinley
Flushing, MI 48435
810 659-9801
Tues. to Sat. 10:30 to 5
Downtown, half block north of Main Street, west side of the street.

31 Luella's Antiques and Things
104 North Maple Street
Flushing, MI 48433
810 659-8955
Tues. to Fri. 11 to 5, Sat. 12 to 5, Sun. 12 to 4
West end of downtown, east side of street, half block north of Main Street.
Small shop; glassware etc.

CLIO

32 Marie's Barn Antiques
G-12213 North Saginaw (M-83)
Clio, MI 48420
810 687-5270
Mon. to Sat. 10 to 5.
West side of street, half mile north of M-57.

Other Antique Shop Directories are available for Western Michigan, Indiana, and the Chicago Metropolitan Area. A Directory will be available for Downstate Illinois late in 1994 or early 1995. Call 616 469-5995 for information.

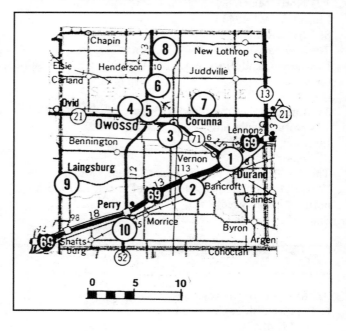

Recommended Points of Interest:
1. Owosso: Curwood Castle and Comstock Cabin, 224
Curwood Castle Drive, 1 block east of M-52. 1922 French
chateau & 1836 cabin. 517 723-6513

Additional Information:
Owosso Chamber of Commerce, 517 723-5149

DURAND   BANCROFT

1 Donna's Cherishables
200 North Saginaw Street
Durand, MI 48429
517 288-3440
Mon. to Fri. 11 to 5; Sat. 11 to 4
Across from Citizens Bank.

2 Roune Galleries
104 South Main Street
Bancroft, MI 48414
517 634-9111
Sign on door says Fri. to Tues. 11 to 6, but call first.
Downtown, west side of street.

CORUNNA

3 Ken's Consignment Resale Shop
M-71 & State Road
Corunna, MI
517 743-3329
Fri. 10 to 9, Sat. 10 to 5:30, Sun. 1 to 5, or by
chance.
Downtown across from Court House, at the traffic light.

OWOSSO

4 Scavenger Hut
114 West Main Street
Owosso, MI 48867
517 725-7200
Mon. to Sat. 10 to 5, Sun. by chance.
Downtown, north side of street, half block west of
Washington. Connects to Town Square Mall.

5 Days Gone By
Town Square Mall
Owosso, MI 48867
517 725-1914; 517 634-5469
Tues. to Thurs. 10:30 to 4:30, Fri. 10:30 to 6, Sat. 11
to 4
Downtown, northwest corner Washington & Main in the
Town Square Mall project.

6 Midtown Antiques Mall
1426 North M-52
Owosso, MI 48867
517 723-8604
Mon. to Sat. 10:30 to 5:30, Sun. 11 to 4:30
East side of the street, north edge of town.
22 dealers.

7 Sharps Rec-Collections
4993 West M-21
Owosso, MI
No telephone listed.
North side of highway, 6.7 miles east of M-52, just west
of Sherman Road.
New & Used Collectibles & antiques.

8 Treasure Chest
M-52
Owosso, MI
517 625-3438; 517 723-4644
Sat., Sun., & Wed. 11 to 5, or by chance.
East side of highway, 5.4 miles north of M-21, just
north of Riley Road.
Used furniture, collectibles, antiques.

LAINGSBURG

9 The Found Object
11600 South Woodbury Road
Laingsburg, MI 48848
517 675-5188
By Appointment.

PERRY

10 Bobbie's Gifts & Collectibles
10980 South M-52
Perry, MI 48872
517 625-7817
Wed. to Sat. 11 to 6, Sun. 12 to 7
One block south of M-52 & I-69 intersection, west side
of street.

Mailing labels available for all Michigan antique shops:
$50.00.   Labels for all Indiana antique shops: $40.00.

Complete Antique Shop Directories
14906 Red Arrow Highway
Lakeside MI 49116
616 469-5995

4.5 CLNTON COUNTY

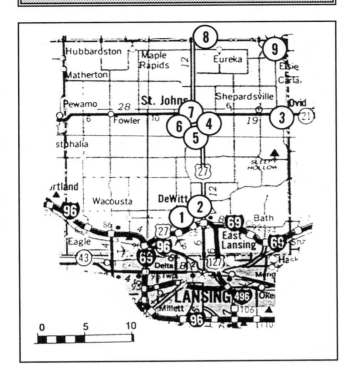

Recommended Points of Interest:
1. St. Johns: Paine-Gillam-Scott Museum, 1860 brick house.
Additional Information:
St. Johns Chamber of Commerce, 517 224-7248

DEWITT

1 Ely's Collectibles
126 North Bridge
DeWitt, MI 48820
517 669-9048
By appointment.
Downtown, southeast corner Bridge & Jefferson Streets.
Primitives, books.

2 Grumpy Bear Antiques
113 West Main Street, downtown
DeWitt, MI 48820
517 669-2327
Thurs. to Sun. 11 to 6

OVID

3 My Little Shop
950 East M-21
Ovid, MI 48866
517 834-2520
Tues. to Sat. 11 to 5, Sun. 12 to 4:30
South side of highway, 1/2 mile east of Ovid.
Primitives, flea market items, etc.

ST. JOHNS

4 Wildflower Antiques
800 East State Street
St. Johns, MI 48879
517 224-6505
Mon. to Fri. 1 to 6
State is the street on the south side of the Court House;
2 blocks east of Business U.S. 27.

5 Irrer Antiques
201 West McConnell
St. Johns, MI 48879
517 224-4085
Every Day 11 to 6, or by appointment.
White house, southwest corner Church & McConnell
Streets; 7 blocks west of 27 or 2 blocks south of 21.

6 Antiques & Collectibles
601 West Cass Street
St. Johns, MI 48879
517 224-3864
Mon. to Sat. 11 to 6, or by appointment.
Cass is the street north of the Court House.
Small shop in garage attached to house.

7 Jerry Nickel Antiques
Lansing Street
St. Johns, MI 48879
517 224-6248
By appointment.
1300 N. Lansing Street (3 blocks west of Clinton), north
of town.

8 County Line Antiques

2021 S County Line Rd
St. Johns, MI 48879
517 224-6285, res: 517 838-2526
Thurs. to Mon. 10 to 5:30
Northeast corner U.S. 27 & County Line Road, 8 miles
north of St. Johns.
Nice general line of antiques.

ELSIE

9 Melvin Antiques & Clock Shop

8401 Island Road
Elsie, MI 48831
517 862-4322
Daily 10 to 8 by chance or appointment.
3/4 mile west of stoplight on West Main Street.

TIER 5:
THE MICHIGAN 46 ROUTE

5.1 SANILAC COUNTY

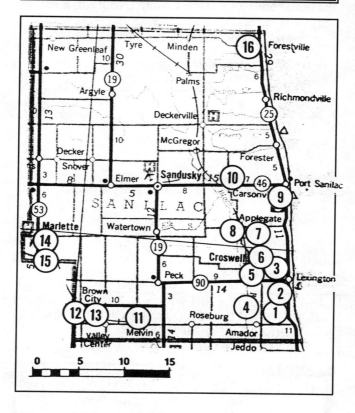

Recommended Points of Interest:
1. Sanilac: Sanilac Historical Museum, 228 South Ridge
(M-25).   1872 Victorian mansion & log cabin.
Additional Information:
Sandusky Chamber of Commerce, 810 648-4445

LEXINGTON

1 Discover An Antique
6901 Mortimer Line
Lexington, MI 48450
810 359-8972   Open by appointment.
South on M-25 2.5 miles, west on Mortimer Line .5
mile; north side of the road.

Village House Antiques
5666 Main St.
Lexington, MI 48450
Open Weekends Or By Chance

Clair & Elva Mills

359-7733
399-1975

2 Village House Antiques
5666 Main Street
Lexington, MI 48450
810 359-7733
Weekends or by chance.
West side of street, 2 blocks south of light.

3 Time Will Tell
7245 Huron Ave.
Lexington, MI 48450
810 359-2046
Sat. & Sun. 11 to 5
Half block west of Route M-25, north side of M-90.

CROSWELL

4 Antiques In The Pointe
1800 Mortimer Line
Croswell, MI 48422
Home: 810 977-5985; shop: 810 378-5251
Weekends only by chance or appointment.
From M-90 south on Brown Road to Mortimer, west on
Mortimer 1/2 mile, south side of road.

5 Granny's Attic
27 South Howard Street
Croswell, MI 48422
810 679-2975
Sun. & Mon. 11 to 5; also Wed. in summer.
East side of street, 3 blocks north of M-90.

6 Allen Dodd Primitives-Furniture
4691 Croswell Road
Croswell, MI 48422
810 679-2936
Sat. & Sun. 10 to 6 or call anytime.
Croswell Road is at the east end of town; north of
Harrington Road, east side of street.

APPLEGATE

7 Julia Ostrowski Antiques
4762 Main Street
Applegate, MI 48401
810 633-9479
Sun. 10 to 5, or by appointment.
Downtown, at "The Old Bank".

8 Carol's Antiques & Treasures
4749 Main Street
Applegate, MI 48401
810 679-3399
Sun. & Wed. 10 to 5, or by chance or appointment.
Northwest corner, center of town.

PORT SANILAC

9 Liberty Rose Antiques
56 South Ridge (M-25)
Port Sanilac, MI 48469
810 622-9500; 810 628-6616
May to Sept.: Sat. & Sun. 10 to 5
West side of the street.

CARSONVILLE

10 Carriage House Antiques
5351 East Sanilac
Carsonville, MI 48419
810 657-9433
Weekends by appointment.
3 1/2 miles west of Port Sanilac.

MELVIN

11 Hidden Valley Antiques
2176 Salisbury
Melvin, MI 48454
810 346-3003
Open by chance or appointment.
1st road South of Galbraith Line, east of Shephard Road.

BROWN CITY

12 Nugent's Antiques
4227 Main Street (M-90)
Brown City, MI 48416
810 346-2254
Mon. to Sat. 10 to 6; Sun. 12 to 6
Downtown, south side of street.

13 Timeless Creations
Main Street
Brown City, MI 48416
810 346-3747
Mon. to Sat. 10 to 6; Sun. 12 to 6
Downtown, south side of street.
19,000 square feet.

MARLETTE

14 Victorian Expressions
3031 Main Street (Van Dyke; M-53)
Marlette, MI 48453
517 635-3939 or 517 635-3890
Mon. to Sat. 9 to 6
Downtown, east side of street.
Cards, gifts, some antiques in back.

15 Treasures Of The Heart Mall
3105 Van Dyke (Main Street; M-53)
Marlette, MI 48453
517 635-7007
Daily 10 to 5
South edge of downtown, east side of street.
10 dealers.

5.1 Sanilac County - continued

FORESTVILLE

16 The Farm House
7914 Lake Road
Forestville, MI 48434
517 864-5534
May 30 to Oct. 1: Every Day 11 to 5
Behind the Catholic Church.

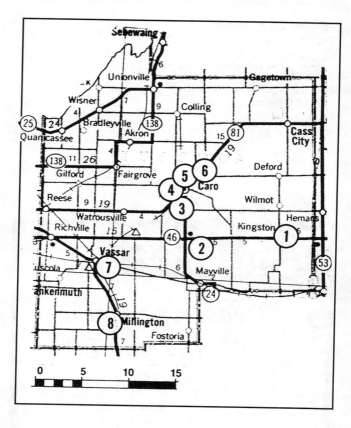

Recommended Points of Interest:
Vassar: Slow-water canoeing on the Cass River, and
hunting and hiking in the 3,000 acre Vassar State Game
Area.

Additional Information:
Tuscola County Tourism Council, 517 673-2849.

KINGSTON

1 Barron's Antiques
5969 State Street (M-46)
Kingston, MI 48741
517 683-2750
Mon. to Sat. 10 to 6
Downtown, north side of street.

CARO

2 Thumb's-Up Antique Village & Village Diner
1220 East Sanilac Road (M-46)
Caro, MI 48723
517 673-5533
Daily 8 to 5, Mon. & Thurs. to 7
One mile East of M-24, south side of highway.
Restaurant in front, antiques in back.

3 Quilt Talk-Antiques
209 North State
Caro, MI 48723
517 673-7994
Tues. to Thurs. 10 to 5:30, Fri. 10 to 8, Sat. 9 to 2
Downtown, north side of street, just east of Lincoln.

4 Next Door Neighbor
218 North State
Caro, MI 48723
517 673-3200
Mon. to Fri. 9 to 5:30, Sat. 9 to 5; Fri. to 8
Downtown, south side of street, middle of block.
Gifts, crafts, country furniture, accessories, a few
antiques.

5 Gallery Unique
1333 East Caro Road
Caro, MI 48723
517 673-5118
Summer: Mon. to Sat. 10 to 6;
Winter: Wed. to Sat. 10 to 6
Northeast end of town, northwest side of highway, a
mile and a half northeast of M-24. Shed next to house.

6 Just Plain Janes
North State
Caro , MI 48723
No phone listed.
Open by chance.
Northeast side of town, northwest side of street.
Antiques, crafts, and things.

VASSAR

7 Pretty By Pam
145 East Huron Avenue (M-15)
Vassar, MI 48768
517 823-2099
Mon. to Fri. 9 to 5; Sat. 9 to 5
Downtown
Flowers, cards, gifts and antiques.

MILLINGTON

8 Country Shops
8600 State Street
Millington, MI 48746
517 871-3523
Mon. to Sat. 10 to 5, Sun. 12 to 5; closed Sun. & Mon.
Jan. to Mar.
West side of street, just south of downtown.
Gifts, crafts, country collectibles & antiques in main
building, antiques (some in the rough) in barn in back.

BAY CITY, MIDLAND, SAGINAW

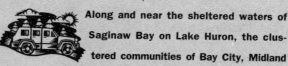

Along and near the sheltered waters of
Saginaw Bay on Lake Huron, the clus-
tered communities of Bay City, Midland
and Saginaw (about an hour's drive northwest of Detroit)
were founded during the area's 19th-century lumber boom.
They remain vital commercial centers, but all also cater to
vacationers who travel to this area of the state's "thumb."

5.3 SAGINAW COUNTY

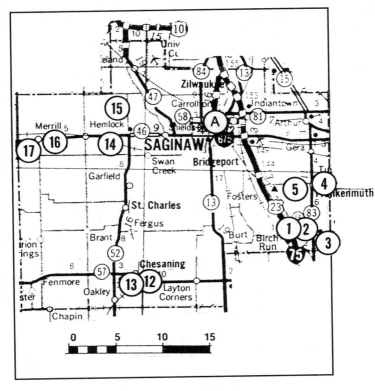

A. Saginaw: 6 to 11 (See Detail Map)

Recommended Points of Interest:
1. Japanese Cultural Center and Tea House, 1315 South
Washington. 517 759-1648, 517 759-1531; May to Dec.
2. Saginaw: Green Point Nature Center, 3010 Maple Street.

Additional Information:
Saginaw County Conv. & Tourism Bureau, 517 752-7164

BIRCH RUN

1 The Collector's Corner and Aunt Mary's Attic
11970 S. Gera Road (M-83)
Birch Run, MI 48415
517 624-9161
Sat. 10 to 6, Sun. to Fri. 12 to 5
Northwest corner Gera & Birch Run Roads; 2 miles east
of I-75 Exit 136.

2 The Collector's Corner II
11900 S. Gera Road (MI Route 83)
Birch Run, MI 48415
517 624-4388
Sat. 10 to 6, Sun. to Fri. 12 to 5
Shares parking lot with The Collector's Corner and Aunt Mary's Attic; Collector's Corner II is the red building at north side of parking lot.

FRANKENMUTH

3 Redbeard's Antiques & Collectibles
12025 South Gera Road
Frankenmuth, MI 48634
517 624-5211; 810 653-6070,
Daily 10 to 6
Southeast corner Gera & Birch Run Roads, south of Frankenmuth.

4 Schoolhaus Antiques
245 South Main Street
Frankenmuth, MI 48734
517 652-3688
Summer: Mon. to Sat. 10 to 5; Sun. 12 to 5
Winter: Sun. to Fri. 12 to 5; Sat. 11 to 5
Downtown, Top of the Hill, In Schoolhaus Square shopping complex, east side of street.
Formerly Old Bank Antiques.

5 B-C Antiques
8470 West Tuscola Road
Frankenmuth, MI 48734
517 652-2116
Almost any time by chance.
3 miles west of downtown; shop in building behind the house.

Detail Map: Saginaw

A. Old Saginaw City: 6 to 9

SAGINAW

6 Antique Warehouse
1910 North Michigan Ave.
Saginaw, MI 48602
517 755-4343
Mon. to Sat. 10 to 5, Sun. 12 to 5
1.4 miles north of Old Saginaw City; From I-75 take I-675 Exit at Davenport St., left on Hill St., left on Genesee to Michigan, right 1/2 block, east side of street.
70 dealers, 30,000 square feet.

7 A Cut Above Antiques
218 South Hamilton
Saginaw, MI 48602
517 790-1210
Tues. to Fri. 11 to 5
East side of street, 2 blocks south of Court Street.
Glassware, toys, holiday items, etc.

8 Looking Glass Antiques
406 Court Street
Saginaw, MI 48602
517 790-7477
Mon. to Sat. 10 to 5
North side of Street, between Michigan Avenue and the
river.

9. Antique Market Place
410 Court Street
Saginaw, MI 48602
517 799-4110
Mon. to Sat. 10 to 5

10 Adomaitis Antiques
412 Court Street
Saginaw, MI 48600
517 790-7469
Mon. to Sat. 10:30 to 5

11 Court Street Antiques
1309 Court
Saginaw, MI 48602
517 799-1481
By chance or appointment.
Southwest side of street, between Michigan and Bay.

CHESANING

12 Oldies But Goodies
734 West Brady Street
Chesaning, MI 48616
517 845-2303
Mon. to Sat. 9 to 5; Sun. 12 to 4
2 blocks north of the Bonnie Mill Inn.
4.500 square feet.

13 Fancy That Antiques & Uniques
324 West Broad
Chesaning, MI 48616
517 845-7775; 800-752-0532 Outside MI;
FAX: 517 845-4190
Mon. to Sat. 10 to 6; Sun. 12 to 5
Winter: Tues. to Thurs. & Sat. 11 to 5 Sun. 12 to 5
Downtown, on the Boulevard, in Mission style mansion.

HEMLOCK

14 Ron's Antiques
12025 Gratiet Road
Hemlock, MI 48626
517 642-8479
Mon. to Sat. 11 to 4
In old school house at Gleaner Road, East of Hemlock, south side of highway.

15 Pine Grove Antiques & Collectibles
12751 Frost Road
Hemlock, MI 48626
517 642-8667
Fri. & Sat. 11 to 5
From Hemlock: east on M-46 to Orr Road, north on Orr 2 miles to Frost, then east 1/4 mile; south side of road. Restored furniture & general line.

MERRILL

16 Lost Dreams Nostalgia
120 East Saginaw (M-46)
Merrill, MI 48637
517 842-5713
Sat. & Sun. 9 to 5
Downtown, north side of street.
Coca Cola; James Dean; 1950's & 60's.

17 Tillie's Treasures
M-46 West
Merrill, MI 48637
517 643-7516
Sat. & Sun. 10 to 5; closed Easter, Christmas, and 3 weekends after Christmas.
3/4 mile west of Merrill, south side of highway.

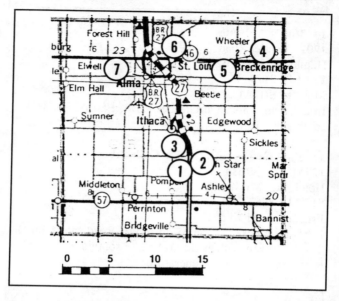

Recommended Points of Interest:
1. Alma: Pine River Park, nature trails.

Additional Information:
Alma Chamber of Commerce, 517 463-5525

ITHACA

1 My Sister's Closet
1355 E. Grant Road
Ithaca, MI 48847
517 838-4096
Summer: Every day 10 to 6; Winter: Every day 10 to 5
West side of U.S. 27, 5 miles south of Buchanan Road,
2 mi north of M-57.
Gifts, glassware, pottery

2 North Star Trader
3036 South Bagley Road, U.S. 27
Ithaca, MI 48847
517 875-4341 or 517 838-4409
Daily 11 to 5; closed Wed.
West side of highway, 3 miles south of Ithaca.
Used furniture, oak reproductions, & antiques; 25% of
the items are antiques.

3 Countryside Antiques
2024 South Bagley, U.S. 27
Ithaca, MI 48847
517 875-2349
Summer: Mon. to Sat. 10 to 6, Sunday 12 to 6;
Winter: Mon. to Sat. 10 to 5, Sunday 12 to 5
West side of U.S. 27, north of Buchanan Road.

WHEELER

4 Auntie Q's
8150 N. Mason
Wheeler, MI 48662
517 842-5862
Summer: Mon. to Sat. 10 until dark, Sun. 11 until dark;
Winter: Tues. to Sat. 10 to 5, Sun. 11 to 5.
Northeast corner Mason Road & M-46 between Merrill and Breckenridge.

BRECKENRIDGE

5   BJ's Antiques & Coins
222 Saginaw
Breckenridge , MI 48615
517 842-5572
Mon. to Fri. 9 to 5; Sat. 9 to 3
Downtown, next to Village Pro Hardware, south side of
street.

ST. LOUIS

6   Mary's Memories
603 East Washington
St. Louis , MI 48880
517 681-2286
Wed. to Fri. 10 to 5; Sat. 10 to 2
North side of street between Euclid and Hubbard, east
side of St. Louis.   There is a turn-around with a grass
lawn in front of the shop.

ELWELL

7 MacLachlan House Antiques
6482 N Pingree Rd
Elwell, MI 48832
517 463-1512
May to December: Sat. & Sun. 12 to 5; or by
appointment.
Downtown, southeast corner Kates Drive & Pingree
Road.
Vintage radio and phonograph items, etc.

TIER 6:
SAGINAW BAY

6.1 HURON COUNTY

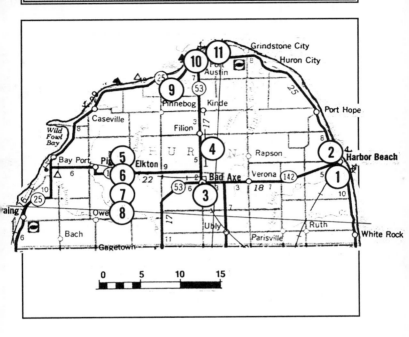

Recommended Points of Interest:
1. Port Austin: Port Crescent State Park, M-43, 4 miles east.
2. Huron City: House of the Seven Gables, occupied by same family since 1881.

Additional Information:
Huron County Tourist Information, 517 269-6431

HARBOR BEACH

1 McGray's Antiques
230 State Street (M-142)
Harbor Beach, MI 48441
517 479-3713
Summer: Mon. to Sat. 10 to 6, Sun. 12 to 6;
Winter: Thurs. to Sat. 10 to 6, Sun. 12 to 6
South side of street.

2 Margaret's Antiques
18 State Street
Harbor Beach, MI 48441
517 479-9835
Wed., Fri., Sat. 10 to 5; closed Jan. & Feb.
South side of street.

BAD AXE

3 Antiques
160 East Huron Street
Bad Axe, MI 48413
517 269-9080
By appointment.
Downtown, southeast corner Huron & Point Crescent, next
to The Doll House, in former Ben Franklin store.
Stop at The Doll House for information.

4 The Old Mill Antiques
M-53
Bad Axe, MI
517 269-9254
Sat. 12 to 5, Sun. 12 to 4, or by appointment.
3.9 miles north of Bad Axe, southeast corner M-53 &
Crown Road.
Antiques, collectibles, gifts, and an old-fashioned ice cream
parlor in season.

ELKTON

5 Elkton Depot Antiques
76 North Main
Elkton, MI 48731
517 375-2739;   517 868-9730
May to Nov.: Tues. to Sun. 12 to 4
North of downtown, east side of street.
Building was for sale at time of site visit.

6 McKenzie's Gifts & Antiques
48 North Main Street
Elkton, MI 48731
517 375-2750
Mon. to Sat. 9 to 5
Downtown, east side of street.

7 Antiques & More
36 North Main Street
Elkton, MI 48731
517 375-2426
Fri. & Sat. 9:30 to 5
Downtown
10 dealers

8 The Country Flea Market
34 North Main Street
Elkton, MI 48731
517 678-4370
Fri. & Sat. 9 to 5
Downtown

PORT AUSTIN

9 The Old Oak Shop
7040 Oak Beach Road
Port Austin, MI 48467
517 738-5258
Summer only: Sat. & Sun. 10 to 5
Nine miles west from Port Austin on M-25, 1/2 block east
on Oak Beach Road; north side of road across from trailer
park.

10 Timeless Treasures
Spring Street
Port Austin, MI 48467
No telephone listed.
By chance.
North side of street, just west of M-33, in same building as
Huron Realty.

11 Olde Village Peddler
120 West Spring Street
Port Austin, MI 48467
517 738-6445
By chance.
South side of street, 2 blocks east of M-53, across from
Eagles Marina.

6.2 BAY COUNTY

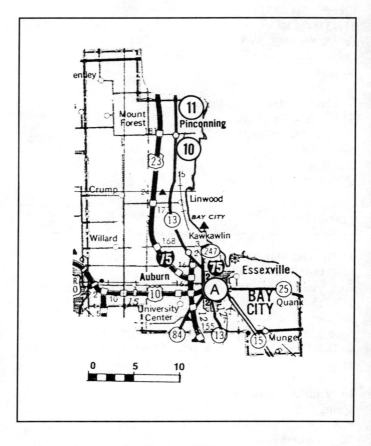

A. Bay City: 1 to 9 (See Detail Map)

Recommended Points of Interest:
1. Bay City: City Hall & Chmielewska Tapestry, 301
Washington Avenue. 1894 Romanesque building;   Council
Chamber has 31 foot long woven tapestry.
2. Bay City: Jennison Nature Center and Tobico Marsh, I-75 to
Beaver Road exit, 5 miles east.   517 667-0717
3. Bay City: Historical Museum of Bay County, 321 Washington
Avenue, 517 893-5733
4. Pinconning: Just south of town is Deer Acres, a park with a
train safari and beautiful surroundings.

Additional Information:
Bay County Convention & Visitors Bureau, 517 893-1222
Bay Area Chamber of Commerce, 517 893-4567
Pinconning Area Chamber of Commerce, 517 879-2816

164

Detail Map: Bay City

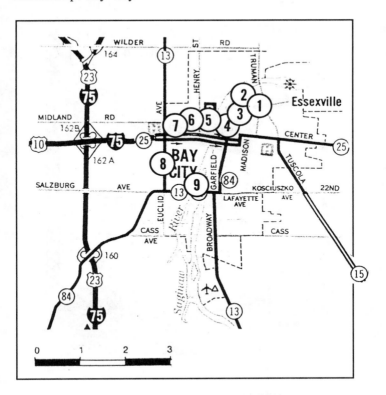

BAY CITY

1 Hen in the Holly
110 Third Street
Bay City, MI 48708
517 895-7215
Summer: Mon. to Sat. 10 to 4, Sun. 12 to 4;
Winter: Tues. to Sat. 10 to 4
South side of the street between Water & Washington.
Antiques and folk art.

2 Ye Olde Lamp Shoppe
108 Third Street
Bay City, MI 48706
517 892-7569
By chance or appointment.
Downtown, south side of the street between Water &
Washington, just east Bay City Antiques Center.

MICHIGAN'S LARGEST!
AAA "Best Antique Mall"

Open 7 days
Weekdays 10 - 5; Sundays Noon - 5
Fridays til 9:00

Bay City Antiques Center

THIRD & WATER
DOWNTOWN BAY CITY
517 893-1116

3 Bay City Antiques Center
1010 North Water Street
Bay City, MI 48708
517 893-1116
Mon. to Sat. 10 to 5, Fri. till 9; Sun. 12 to 5
Southeast corner Third & Water Streets. From I-75 take
Exit 162-A to downtown, take the 1st left after the river
(i.e. Saginaw Street), go 6 blocks north to 3rd Street, then
left 1 block to Water Street, then left. Entrance is under the
blue awning.
43,000 square feet, expanding in 1994 to 55,000 square
feet. Snack shop in the mall.

4 Little House Creations
924 North Water
Bay City, MI 48706
517 893-6771
Mon. to Sat. 10 to 5, Sun. 12 to 4
Downtown, near the Bay City Antiques Center.

(Check out the candy & nut shop at NWC 3rd & Water)

5 Owl Antiques
703 East Midland Street
Bay City, MI 48706
517 892-1105
Tues. to Sat. 10 to 5
North side of street, 2 blocks west of the river in the
Historic West Side Midland District, one block south of the
Vermont Street bridge. Go south on Walnut after crossing
bridge.

6 Eichorns Antiques
300 West Midland Street
Bay City, MI 48706
517 686-2217
By chance.
Houst at the northwest corner Chilson & Midland Streets.
Small shop in the front room of the house.

7 Butterfield Antiques
605 West Midland Street
Bay City, MI 48706
517 684-3229
Tues. 9 to 5, other days by appointment.
Victorian house at southeast corner Midland Street & Alp
Avenue, 2 blocks east of Euclid.
Only a tiny sign on a column.

8 Everybody's Attic
1217 South Euclid
Bay City, MI 48706
517 684-6674
Every Day 10 to 5:30
East side of the street; a group shop.

9 Edelweiss Antiques
204 Saltzberg Street
Bay City, MI 48706
517 684-6079
Summer by chance.
North side of street, just west of the bridge, 1 block west of
Winona Street.

PINCONNING

10 Country Folk Creations
3726 N. Huron Road (M-13)
Pinconning, MI 48650
517 879-4328
Summer only: Wed. to Mon. 10 to 5
East side of the highway, 1/2 mile south of light.
Mostly crafts.

11 Red Barn Antiques
(Down Memory Lane Antiques)
M-13
Pinconning, MI 48650
517 892-4823; 517 879-4435
Fri. to Mon. 11 to 6
West side of highway, north of town.

6.3 MIDLAND COUNTY

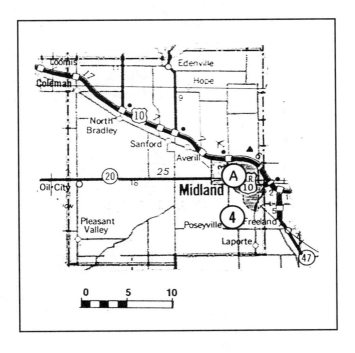

A. Midland: 1 to 3 (See Detail Map)

Recommended Points of Interest:
1. Midland: Dow Gardens, 1018 West Main. 517 631-2677

Additional Information:
Midland County Conv. & Visitors Bureau, 517 839-9901.

MIDLAND

1 Corner Cupboard
2108 East Wheeler Road
Midland, MI 48640
517 835-6691
By chance.
Small building next to house, south side of the street
midway between Swede and Waldo Streets.

Detail Map: Midland

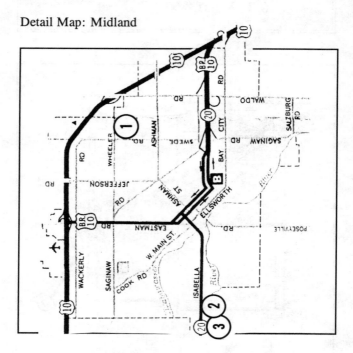

2 Pickett Fence Antiques
476 East Isabella (M-20)
Midland, MI 48640
517 631-4108
By chance or appointment.
South side of highway, 5 miles west of Midland.

3 Carolyn's Country Cupboard
484 Isabella
Midland, MI 48640
517 832-0855
Thurs. to Mon. 10:30 to 5
South side of highway, 5 miles west of Midland, next to
Pickett Fence Antiques.

4 D.A.D.'s Antiques
3004 Poseyville Road
Midland, MI 48640
517 835-7483
Wed. to Sun. 10 to 4
Southwest corner Poseyville & Freeland Roads, 6 miles
south of downtown.

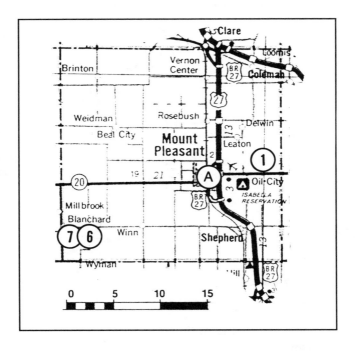

A. Mount Pleasant: 2 to 5 (See Detail Map)

Recommended Points of Interest:
1. Mount Pleasant: Center for Cultural and Natural History, Central Michigan University. 517 774-3829

Additional Information:
Isabella County Conv. & Visitors Bureau, 517 774-3829

MT. PLEASANT

1 Schoolhouse Antiques
8995 East Pickard (M-20)
Mt. Pleasant , MI 48858
517 772-4660
May to Dec.: Fri. to Mon. 12 to 5;
Jan. to April: Fri. to Sun. 12 to 5
Northwest corner Loomis & Pickard (M-20), 5 miles
east of Mt. Pleasant.
5 dealers

Detail Map: Mount Pleasant

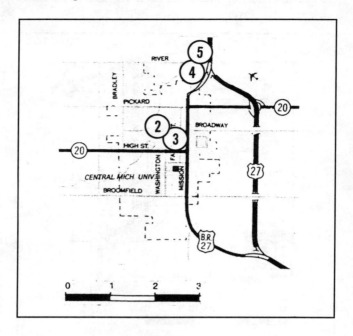

2   Ditman Shoes & Antiques
133 East Broadway
Mt. Pleasant , MI 48858
517 773-4652
By chance or appointment.
Downtown, north side of street.

3   Our Vintage Shop
620 South Mission (Business 27)
Mt. Pleasant , MI 48858
517 773-5116
Mon 11 to 4, Tues. to Sat. 10 to 5:30, Sun. by chance.
West side of highway, across road from and a little
north of Ric's Supermarket.

4   Valley Resale
Old 27 and River Rd
Mt Pleasant , MI 48858
517 772-5268
Mon. to Fri 10:30 to 5:30; Sat. by chance; usually open.
South side of River Road just east of Old 27, 1 mile
north of Mt. Pleasant.
Glass, pottery, antiques and used furniture.

5 Riverside Antiques & Collectibles
993 S Mission Road
Mt Pleasant , MI 48858
517 773-3946
Mon. to Sat. 11 to 5; Sun. by chance.
North on Old 27, east side of road just north of river.
Dried flowers, candles, primitives, collectibles and gifts.

BLANCHARD

6 Johnson's Junque
424 Main St
Blanchard , MI 49310
517 561-2075
April to Dec.: Thurs. to Sat 10 to 5
South side of street, east end of downtown.

7 Loafer's Glory
431 Main Street
Blanchard , MI 49310
517 561-2020; (517 831-4264 res.)
April to Dec.: Tues. to Sat. 10 to 5;
Feb. & Mar.: Thurs. to Sat. 10 to 4; Closed Jan.
Downtown, north side of street.
Most antiques are on the second floor.

See the **Introduction** for a description of how the
counties are arranged in this Directory. Also, see the
Index of Counties and the **Index of Towns and Cities**
in the front of the Directory.

It is easy to find what you are looking for once you
know the system of organization.

TIER 7:
MICHIGAN 61 ROUTE

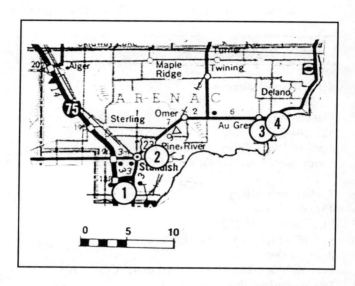

STANDISH

1 J & V Antiques
5108 S. Huron (MI 13)
Standish, MI 48658
517 846-4437
By appointment or chance.
West side of highway, 3 miles south of town. Shed &
barn in back of house.

OMER

2 Quilt Patch Antiques
429 East Center (U.S. 23)
Omer, MI 48749
517 653-2332
May 1 to Nov. 1: Daily 9 to 6; Winter by chance or
appointment.
North side of highway, just east of the railroad tracks.

AU GRES

3 Nick's Wood Shop
134 Michigan Ave.
Au Gres, MI 48703
517 876-7075
April to Oct.: Mon. to Sat. 10 to 6, Sun. 10 to 3, closed
Thurs.;   Nov. to Mar.: by appointment.
One block south of blinker light south of U.S. 23.
Refinishing & antiques.

4 The Second Time Around Antiques
611 Michigan Ave.
Au Gres, MI 48703
517 876-7413
Summer: Every day 10 to 5
At H & H Restaurant & Bakery on U.S. 23 turn south
on Main; go 2 blocks to Michigan and turn left (east).
Big white house surrounded by white picket fence.

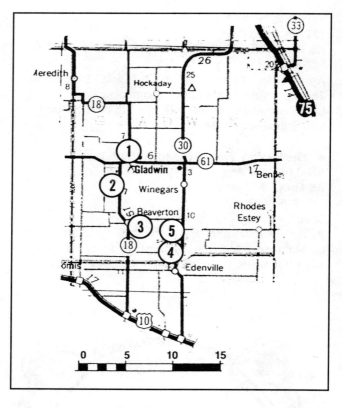

Additional Information:
Gladwin County Chamber of Commerce, 517 426-5451

GLADWIN

1 Passin' Time
225 West Cedar Avenue (the main street)
Gladwin, MI 48624
517 426-7823
Mon. to Fri. 9 to 5, Sat. 9 to 12
Downtown, south side of street.
Clocks and clock & watch repair.

BEAVERTON

2 The Treasure Chest
1722 Highway M-18
Beaverton, MI 48612
No telephone listed.
Weekends only.
House on the west side of highway, 3.1 miles south of
M-61, 4.4 miles north of Beaverton.

3 The Patchwork Quilt Shop
3215 South M-18
Beaverton, MI 48612
517 435-2991; 517 435-3275
Tues. to Sat. 10 to 5
One block south of town, east side of road.
New quilts & antiques.

4 Misty Way Antiques
5137 Dundas Road
Beaverton, MI 48612
517 435-9293 (phone & fax)
Summer only: by chance or appointment.
North from Edenville 1.5 miles on M-30 to Dundas
Road; northwest on Dundas (an unpaved road) 1.1 miles
to the shop; east side of road.
Stained glass, etc.

5 My Sisters' Place
4568 M-30
Beaverton, MI 48612
517 435-4838
Every Day 10 to 5
West side of highway, just south of I.G.A. store, 3
miles north of Edenville.
Gifts, crafts, dried flowers, and antiques.

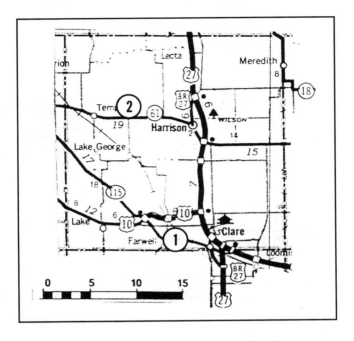

1   Main Street Market Place
175 West Main Street
Farwell , MI 48622
517 588-4466
Mon. to Fri. 11 to 6, closed Thurs.;
Sun. 12 to 5
Downtown, 5 miles west of Clare.

2   Lott's Antiques
(aka Antique Marketing Co.)
7112 West Temple Drive (M-61)
Harrison , MI 48625
616 743-6222
Days and hours not available.
10 miles west of Harrison on north side of highway
M-61.

TIER 8:
THE M-55 ROUTE

8.1 IOSCO COUNTY

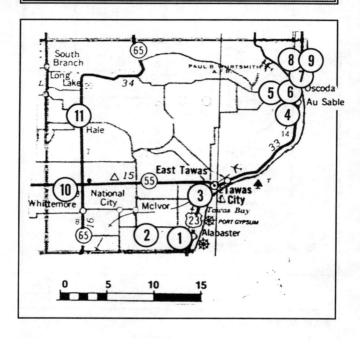

Recommended Points of Interest:
1. Tawas City: Tawas Historical Indian Museum, 1702 U.S. Highway 23. 517 362-5885
2. Oscoda: Gateway to the River Road National Scenic Byway that runs along the south bank of the Au Sable River.
3. Iargo Aprings: 16 miles west of Oscoda on River Road.

Additional Information:
Tawas Area Chamber of Commerce, 517 362-8643

TAWAS CITY

1 Alabaster Corners
2441 Huron
Tawas City, MI 48763
517 362-7777
May 1 to Dec. 31: Every day 10 to 5
West side of highway, 6 miles south of Tawas City.
Gifts, collectibles, antiques, candles, & Christmas shop.

2 Townline Antiques & Collectibles
3707 West Townline Road
Tawas City, MI 48763
517 362-3641
Sat. & Sun. 10 to 5 or by appointment.
At the south edge of Tawas City turn west off U.S. 23
by the Alibi Bar onto Townline Road; go 6 miles; on
south side of road.
Reproductions and antiques.

3 Uncle Winnies
Bruggers Plaza, 304 Lake Street (U.S. 23)
Tawas City, MI 48764
517 362-6644
Mon. to Sat. 10 to 6, Sun. 11 to 4
West side of street 3 blocks south of M-55 in a small
retail plaza.

OSCODA

4 Hobart's Plaza
4219 U.S. 23
Oscoda, MI 48750
517 739-4000
Summer: Every day 10 to 6;
Winter: Fri. to Sun. 11 to 5, or by appointment.
In the back right corner of a complex of buildings, 1.7
miles south of downtown, west side of highway.
Reproductions in the front building, antiques &
collectibles in the back building

5 Riverview Antiques
308 West Dwight
Oscoda, MI 48750
517 739-0363
By chance or appointment.
1 block south and 3 blocks west of downtown traffic
light.
Entrance on the side of the house; no sign; just ring the
door bell.

6 Wooden Nickel Antiques
110 Park Street
Oscoda, MI 48750
517 739-7490
Summer: Daily 12 to 5, (Mon. by chance);
Winter: Fri. to Sun. 12 to 5
2 blocks south and 1/2 block east of downtown traffic light.
Rear building.

7 A Summer Place
118 E. River Road
Oscoda, MI 48750
517 739-8309
May to Oct.: Daily except Mon. 12 to 5;
Nov. & Dec.: Fri. to Sun. 12 to 5, or by appointment.
South side of street, one block east of downtown traffic light.

8 Jaye's Antiques & Collectibles
5737 North U.S. 23
Oscoda, MI 48750
517 739-0363
Thurs. to Mon. 11 to 5; Tues. & Wed. by chance
Small shop in Mini-Street Plaza at north end of the
K-Mart parking lot, 1.5 miles north of downtown.

9 Needful Thing
208 North State Street (U.S. 23)
Oscoda, MI 48750
517 739-0380
Memorial Day to Labor Day: Every Day 10 to 9;
Winter: Wed. to Sat. 11 to 6, Sun. 12 to 6
3 1/2 blocks south of traffic light, east side of street.
Second hand shop: antiques, collectibles, used items.

WHITTEMORE

10 Karry's Antiques
5765 MI 55
Whittemore, MI 48770
517 362-4010
All year 10 to 5, if they are home.
South side of highway, 2 miles east of M-65.
The sign is set way back from the road.

HALE

11 Elsie's Hale Creek Antiques
201 North Washington (M-65)
Hale, MI 48739
517 728-2538; 517 362-4010
May 30 to Labor Day: Thurs. to Mon. 10 to 5;
Sept. & Oct.: Sat. & Sun. 10 to 5
West side of street, one block north of traffic light.

8.2 OGEMAW COUNTY

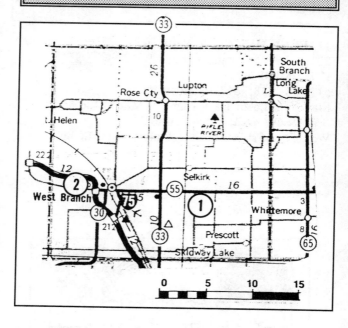

Recommended Points of Interest:
1. Civilian Conservation Corps Museum, U.S. 27 to County Road 200. Open June to Sept. 517 821-6125

PRESCOTT

1 Hilltop House Antiques
2015 East M-55
Prescott, MI 48756
517 345-3540; 517 345-7242
May 1 to Nov. 1: Wed. to Sun. 12 to 5;
Winter: Sat. & Sun. 10 to 5
South side of road at Peterson Road, 4 mi. east of M-33

WEST BRANCH

2 Cocklebur
2161 Pointer Road
West Branch, MI 48661
517 345-7242
April 15 to Dec. 31: Wed. to Fri. 10 to 5, Sat. 10 to 4,
Sun. & holidays by chance.
1 mile west and 1/8 mile south of I-75 Exit 215

8.3 ROSCOMMON COUNTY

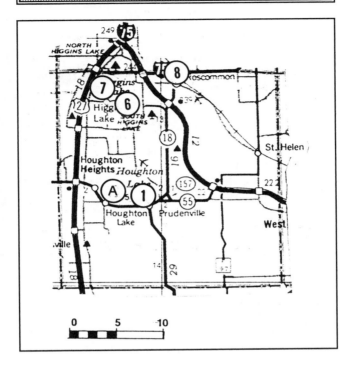

A. Houghton Lake: 2 to 5

PRUDENVILLE

1 The Carousel Shoppe
1460 West Houghton Lake Drive
Prudenville, MI 48651
517 366-5477   Open summer only.
West side of town, northwest corner Iroquois &
Houghton Lake Drive.

HOUGHTON LAKE

2 Rose Arbor Antiques
105 Lake (Knapp Road) Zone 7
Houghton Lake, MI 48629
517 422-4805
April to Dec.: Mon. to Sat. 10 to 5, Sun. 12 to 4
3 miles east of U.S. 27.

3 Berta's Antiques
5800 West Houghton Lake Drive
Houghton Lake, MI 48629
517 422-4104
Summer: Thurs. to Mon. 11 to 5;
Winter: Fri. 11 to 5, Sat. 11 to 5, Sun. 1 to 5, Mon. &
Tues. by appointment.
North side of road one half mile west of Loxley Road,
at Fire Tower Hill Road.

4 Houghton Lake Flea Market
1499 Loxley Road
Houghton Lake, MI 48629
517 422-3011; 517 422-5396
Every Day: 8 to 4, year-round.
East side of road, just south of School Road.
Not a flea market: a large 10,000 square foot good
quality antique shop.

5 Maxine's Antiques
7810 School Road
Houghton Lake, MI 48629
517 422-5751
Summer (April to Dec.): Mon. to Sat. 9 to 4;
Winter: By chance
From Old 27 east on M-55 1.4 miles to Loxley Road,
then south .5 mile to School Road, then east .2 mile;
south side of road.
Good quality furniture.

HIGGINS LAKE

6 Yorty's Antiques
103 Yorty Drive (West Higgins Lake Drive)
Higgins Lake, MI 48627
517 821-9242
Summer
Just east of the U.S. 27 interchange, at Old 27 & Pine
Drive (County Road 104), there is a large sign pointing
the way to local business establishments. From here go
east on Pine Road 1.8 miles to Hillcrest Road, then
north 1.7 miles to West Higgins Lake Drive, then east
1.4 miles. North side of road, across from Higgins
Lake Food Market.

7 Farley's Antique Treasure Trove
10028 West Higgins Lake Drive
Higgins Lake, MI 48627
517 821-6478
Memorial Day to Labor Day: Wed. to Sat. 12 to 6, Sun.
12 to 4
From U.S. 27: Higgins Lake exit east to Old 27, then
north 6 miles. Look for the sign at Haines Street
pointing the way to local business establishments.   Go
east one block, then north one block on West Higgins
Lake Road; east side of street. (Follow signs.)
A shop called Ginger's Collectibles is next door to the
north.

ROSCOMMON

8 T.J.'s Oldies & Goodies
821 Lake Street
Roscommon, MI 48653
517 275-5321
April to Dec.: Mon. to Sat. 10 to 5
Downtown, just north of tracks, west side of street.

TIER 9:
THE MICHIGAN 32 ROUTE

9.1 ALCONA COUNTY

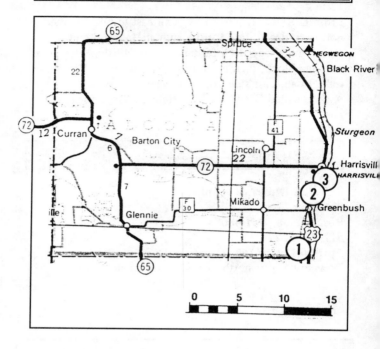

Recommended Points of Interest:
1. Harrisville: Sturgeon Point Lighthouse Museum.

Additional Information:
Huron Shores Chamber of Commerce, 517 724-5107

GREENBUSH

1 The Cedar Closet
4034 U.S. 23 South
Greenbush, MI 48738
517 739-2632 (home phone)
Generally open: Apr. to Nov.: Mon. to Sat. 10 to 4;
Dec. and Mar. Fri. & Sat. 10 to 4; or by appointment
Little house on the west side of the road, 3.5 miles south
of Greenbush.

2 Nuffer's Sunrise Antiques
1823 Sunrise Drive
Greenbush, MI 48738
517 724-6703
By appointment or chance.
At the Greenbush Golf Course, 5 miles north of
Greenbush, go east on Sunrise Drive; go .6 mile to the
end of the road. The shop is in a garage in back of the
house.

HARRISVILLE

3 Mill Creek Antiques
741 U.S. 23
Harrisville, MI 48740
517 724-6475
Mar. to Nov.: Every Say 10 to 6 (closed 1st Fri. of each
month)
East side of road, just south of Springport Golf Course,
1 1/4 mile south of M-62.

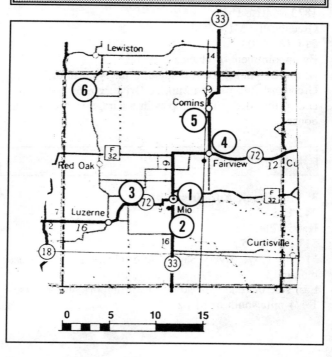

Recommended Points of Interest:
1, Mio: Our Lady of the Woods Shrine and Grotto.
Additional Information:
Mio Chamber of Commerce, 517 826-3331

MIO

1 Granny's Antiques
109 East 8th St.
Mio , MI 48647
517 826-5674
April to Nov.: Daily 11 to 5;   Dec. to March: Sat. 11
to 5, Sun. 11 to 3 or by chance or appointment.
North side of street, 1/2 block east of downtown light.

2 Aunty's Antiques
1743 South MI 33
Mio, MI 48647
517 826-6041
May to Nov.: Daily except Wed. 11 to 5;
Dec. to April: Sat. 11 to 5, Sun. 11 to 4
East side of road, 1.4 miles south of Mio.

3 The Stables
1665 West Kittle Road
Mio, MI 48647
517 826-5454
Thurs. to Mon. 10 to 5
South side of the road, 3.3 miles west of M-33. Kittle
Road is 3 miles north of Mio.
Glassware, quilts, etc.

FAIRVIEW

4 Pettit's Antiques
M-33 Half Mile North of Fairview
Fairview, MI
317 354-2286 (residence)
Mid-April to Oct.: Sat. & Sun. 10 to 5
East side of road, just north of the cemetery.

COMINS

5 Rachel's Neighbor
M-33
Comins, MI 48619
No telephone listed.
Wed. to Sat.
West side of highway, across from post office.
Amish & local crafts, and antiques.

SNYDER LAKE (LEWISTON)

6 Treasure Gallery
County Highway 489
Snyder Lake (Lewiston), MI 49756
517 786-2085
Summer: Daily 11 to 8, closed Wed.;
Winter: Fri. to Sun. 10 to 5
West side of the road, 4 miles south of Lewiston, next
to Snyder Lake Party Store.
Antiques, collectibles, gifts.

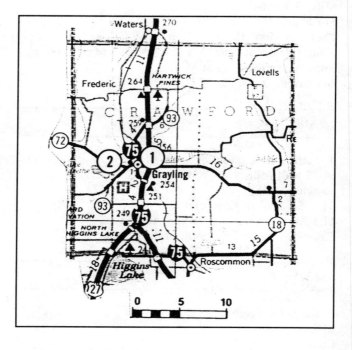

Additional Information:
Grayling Chamber of Commerce, 517 348-2921

GRAYLING

1 Potbelly Antiques
4729 North Down River Road
Grayling, MI 49738
517 348-8578
Apr. to Dec.: Daily 9 to 5; closed winters.
A mile east of Business I-75, south side of street in a
grove of pine trees. Just west of I-75 Exit 256.

2 Ridley's Antiques
6930 M-72 West
Grayling, MI 49738
517 348-5907
March to Jan.: Every day 9 to 6
2 miles west of Grayling, north side of highway.

TIER 10:
SOUTH OF MACKINAC

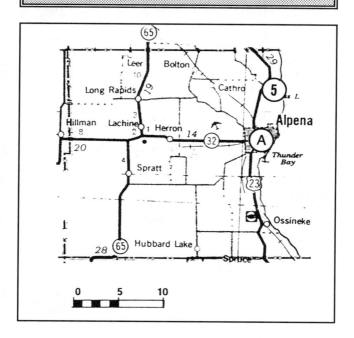

A. Alpena: 1 to 6

Recommended Points of Interest:
1. Alpena: Alpena Sportsmen's Island Wildlife Sanctuary,
U.S. 23 & Long Rapids Road.
2. Alpena: Jesse Besser Museum; American Indian art, tools,
and weapons related to history, & technology of the area. 491
Johnson, n. side of town, 1 bk. east of U.S. 23. 517 356-2202

Additional Information:
Thunder Bay Region Conv. & Visitors Bureau, 517 354-4181

ALPENA

1 Country Cupboard
102 North Second,   Downtown
Alpena, MI 49707
517 356-6635
Mon. to Fri. 10 to 5:30, Sat. 10 to 5

3 Helen's Antiques
127 North 2nd Avenue
Alpena, MI 49707
517 356-3298
Mon. to Sat. 10 to 5:30
East end of downtown, northwest corner River Street &
2nd Avenue.

3 Buck's Antiques
123 North Second Avenue
Alpena, MI 49707
517 356-6635; Res.: 517 356-0940
Summer only.
Downtown, next to Helen's Antiques.

4 Artis Books & Antiques
201 N. Second
Alpena, MI 49707
517 354-3401
Open all year
Downtown

5 Kathy's Bargain Barn
6465 North U.S. 23
Alpena, MI 49707
517 354-3070
Summer only.
East side of highway, 5 miles north of town.

6. Marie's Fabrics & Upholstery
2500 U.S. 23 South
Alpena, MI 49707
517 356-0713
Mon. to Fri. 9 to 5
West side of highway, 3 miles south of downtown.
Very few antiques.

7. The Trading Post
819 West Chisholm (U.S. 23 North)
Alpena, MI 49707
517 354-6036
Summer: Mon. to Fri. 9:30 to 5;
Winter: Mon. to Sat. 9:30 to 5
Even though it is on *West* Chisholm, it is really *north* of
downtown; east side of street.
Coins, some antiques, gas station items.

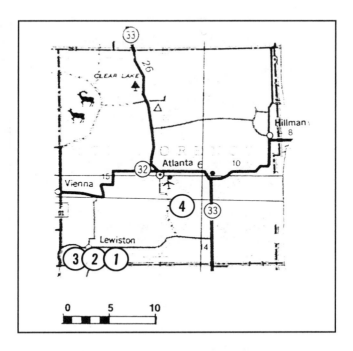

LEWISTON

1 Antique Depot Mall
612 Country Road
Lewiston, MI 49756
517 786-4897
Summer: Daily 11 to 4;
Winter: Thur. to Sun. 11 to 4 by chance.
Corner of County Roads 489 & 612, north side of street,
7 blocks east of town center.

2 Elkhorn Antiques
County Road 612
Lewiston, MI 49756
517 786-4454
Summer: Mon. & Wed. to Sat. 10 to 5, Sun. 11 to 4;
Winter: Fri. & Sat. 10 to 5, Sun. 11 to 4
South side of the road, 4 blocks east of town center.
Gifts, crafts, accessories, antiques.

3 Lewiston Antiqucs
County Road 612
Lewiston, MI 49756
517 786-5812
April 1 to Sept. 30: open daily; Winter: Call for hours.
South side of the street, two blocks west of town center.

ATLANTA

4 Annie's Arc
County Road 487 South
Atlanta, MI 49709
517 785-3929
Summer: Sat. & Sun. 12 to 5; Winter: by Appointment
White house on east side of road, just after the second
90 degree turn, 3 1/4 mile south of Atlanta blinker light.

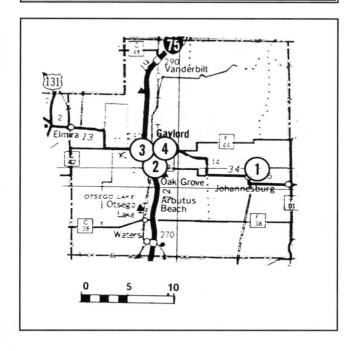

Additional Information:
Gaylord Conv. & Tourism Bureau, 517 732-4002

JOHANNESBURG

1 Cozy Corner Antiques
10816 M-32 East
Johannesburg, MI 49751
517 732-2225
Open Daily 9 to 6; Closed Wed.
Northwest corner of intersection where M-32 turns
south, at flashing light.

GAYLORD

2 The Castle
403 South Otsego
Gaylord, MI 49735
517 732-4665
May to Sept. by chance or appointment.
South of downtown, east side of street.

3 Back Alley Antiques and Collectibles
110 West Main
Gaylord, MI 49735
517 732-8997
Summer: Every day 10 to 8;
Winter: Wed. to Sun. 10 to 4
East end of downtown, north side of street, just west of
Center Street.

4 Country Attic Antiques & Gifts
206 North Center Street
Gaylord, MI 49735
517 732-1142
Mon. to Sat. 10 to 6, Sun. 12 to 5; closed some
Sundays in winter.
From the east end of downtown's Main Street, go north
2 blocks on Center; east side of the street.   Use the
entrance from the parking lot entered from Mitchell St.
Gifts and antiques; courtyard and old log cabin in back.

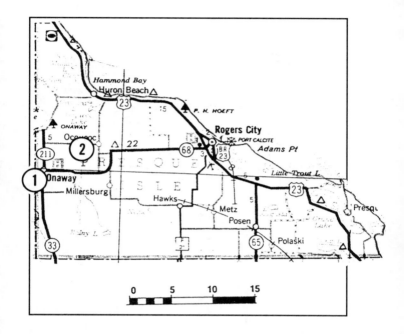

ONAWAY

1 Antiques & More
108 East State
Onaway, MI 49765
517 733-2979
Mon. to Sat. 10 to 5
Eastern end of downtown, south side of street.

2 And Yesterday's Trash
Highway M-33, Hackett Lake Highway
Onaway , MI 49765
517 733-6434
Open Sundays; weekdays by chance.
Four miles south of Onaway to Hackett Lake Highway,
then 6 miles east. Follow signs.
Primitives, old logging tools, etc.

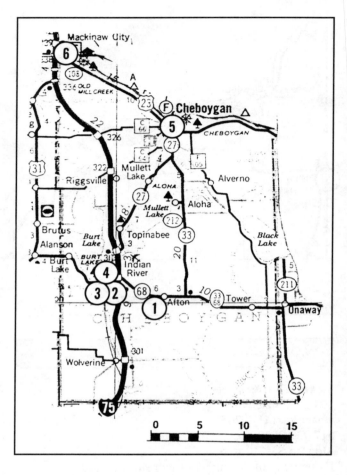

Additional Information:
Cheboygan Chamber of Commerce, 616 627-5841

AFTON

1 Hill Top Antiques
38 Onaway (M-68)
Afton, MI 49705
Every day 10:30 to 4:30
South side of highway, 6 miles east of Indian River,
next to The Country Store.

INDIAN RIVER

2 Bearly Used Antiques & Treasures
6033 East M-68
Indian River, MI 49749
No Telephone listed.
Summer only.
South side of highway, just west of I-75 Exit 310.

3 Books Etc.
4041 South Straits Highway
Indian River, MI 49749
616 238-9008
Mon. to Sat. 10 to 6
In The Plaza, little shopping mall, southeast corner M-68 & South Straits Highway, a half mile west of I-75 Exit 310.
Opened 1994; books & antiques.

4 Antiques
6288 South Avenue
Indian River, MI 49749
Telephone number not available.
Summer only.
Downtown, 1/2 block west of South Straits Highway.

CHEBOYGAN

5 Antiques & Collectibles
211 N. Main Street
Cheboygan, MI 49721
616 627-7237
Mon. to Sat. 10 to 5
Downtown, across from the post office.
Lamp parts & restoration.

MACKINAW CITY

6 A Touch Of Glass & Antiques
226 East Central Avenue
Mackinaw City, MI 49721
616 436-7060
May 1 to Oct. 31: 10 a.m. to 10 p.m. every day
In the Village Square.

TIER 11:
THE UPPER PENINSULA

11.01 MACKINAC COUNTY
11.02 CHIPPEWA COUNTY

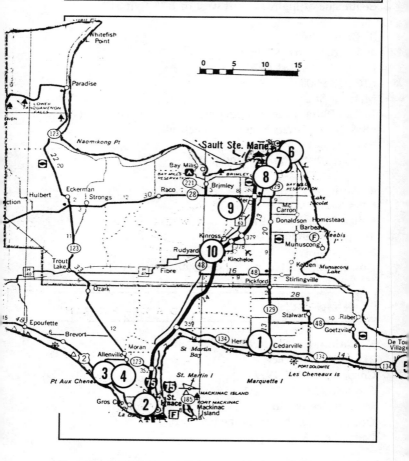

Recommended Points of Interest:
1. Sault Ste. Marie: S.S. Valley Camp and Maritime Museum, Johnston & Water Streets. 906 632-3658
2. St. Ignace: Castle Rock, 3 miles north on Business I-75.
3. Paradise: Tahquamenon Falls State Park. 906 492-3415

Additional Information:
Sault Area Chamber of Commerce, 906 632-3301
St. Ignace Chamber of Commerce, 906 643-8717

CEDARVILLE

1 The Woodshed Gift Shop
M-134 & M-129
Cedarville, MI 49719
906 484-3002
May to Dec.: Mon. to Sat. 10 to 5;
Jan. to Apr.: Fri. & Sat. 10 to 5
1/2 block south of light.

ST. IGNACE

2 Miss Ellen's Mercantile
404 North State Street
St. Ignace, MI check zip
906 643-9274
By chance.
Downtown, west side of street, 1/2 block south of
Goudreau.

3 Anchor In Antiques
2122 West US 2
St. Ignace, MI 49781
906 643-8112; Res.: 906 643-9917
May to Sep: 10 to 5, Closed Wednesday
Oct. to Apr: By chance or appointment.
8 miles west of St. Ignace, north side of highway.
Emphasis on Great Lakes Nautical Items.

4. Superior Paper Company
2122 West U.S. 2 - Unit 1
St. Ignace, MI 49781
906 643-8122
Memorial Day to Labor Day: Thurs. to Tues. 10 to 5
In back of Anchor In Antiques; U.S. 2 west of St.
Ignace.
Military & paper collectibles.

DE TOUR VILLAGE - Chippewa County

5 Log Cabin Antiques & Collectibles
637 Ontario Street, across from the marina.
De Tour Village, MI 49725
906 297-2502
May to Oct.: Mon. to Sat. 9 to 5
No crafts or reproductions.

SAULT STE. MARIE

6 Gran & Gramps Antiques & Collectibles
506 East Portage Avenue
Sault Ste. Marie, MI 49783
906 632-4256
June 1 to Sept. 30: Mon. to Sat. 12 to 6
Winter: Sat. 12 to 6
East on Portage Street 5 blocks; south side of street.

7 Hoffman's Antique Shoppe
514 Emeline Street
Sault Ste. Marie, MI 49783
906 632-0906; res.: 906 632-8769
April to Dec.: Mon. to Sat. 10 to 6;
Jan. to March: Thurs. to Sat. 11 to 5
From Ashman Street: west on Portage 1/2 mile to
Magazine Street, then south 1 block to Emeline Street.

8 La Galerie
1420 Ashmun Street
Sault Ste. Marie, MI 49783
906 635-1044
Mon. to Sat. 10 to 5
Southwest corner Sixth Ave. & Ashmun, south of
downtown, on I-75 Business Spur.

BRIMLEY

9 Willow Grove Farms
M-28
Brimley, MI 49715
906 248-5168
April to Dec. 31: Thurs. to Sun. 11 to 5
4 miles west of I-75, south side of highway, down a
long dirt road.
Antiques, herbs, flowers.

RUDYARD

10 Northern Heritage Antiques & Collectibles
Tilson Road
Rudyard, MI 49780
906 478-3507
May 14 to Oct. 15: Tues. to Sat. 10 to 5
From I-75 west to stop sign, then north one mile.

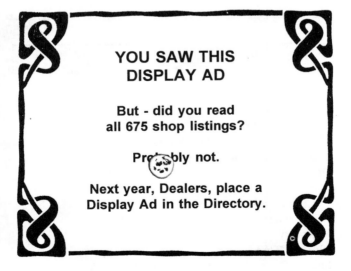

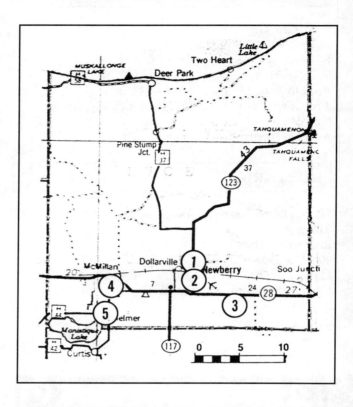

NEWBERRY

1 Antiques By Donelle
101 East John Street
Newberry, MI 49868
906 293-8044; res.: 906 586-9544
Tues. to Fri. 10 to 5, or by appointment; closed March.
Downtown

2 Country Gallery
607 Newberry Avenue (MI Route 123)
Newberry , MI 49868
906 293-8262
June to Oct.: Mon to Sat. 9 a.m. to 10 p.m.;
Winter: Mon. to Fri. 8 to 6, Sat. 9:30 to 6
South of downtown, east side of street.
Mostly gifts, some antiques.

3 Sage River Trading Post
M-28, Route 1 Box 644
Newberry, MI 49868
906 293-5285
June to Oct.: Mon. to Sat. 9 to 5
7 miles west of M-123, south side of highway.
Used items & some antiques.

McMILLAN

4 Calico Cat
Route H-33
McMillan, MI 49853
906 586-3918
May to Sept.: Every Day 9 to 6
West side of road, 3 miles north of Curtis.

5 Farmhouse Antiques
County Road 438
McMillan, MI 49853
906 293-8972
Every day: 10 to 8
South from McMillan on H-33 to Co. Rd. 438, west two
miles on 438; south side of road.

MIKE and PHYLLIS FRENCH
(906) 293-8792

Farmhouse Antiques
Buy, Sell or Trade

Rt. 3, Box 2279
McMillan, MI 49853

Seasonal Hours or
By Appointment

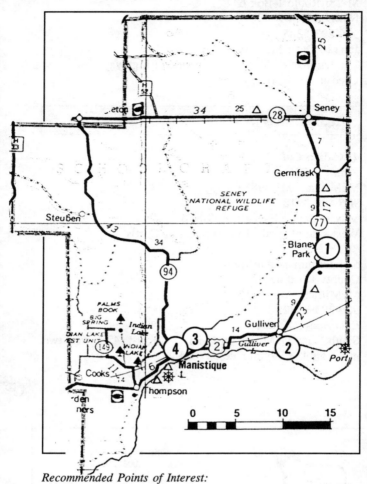

11.04 SCHOOLCRAFT COUNTY

Recommended Points of Interest:
1. Manistique: Palms Book State Park.

Additional Information:
Schoolcraft County Chamber of Commerce, 906 341-5010

BLANEY PARK

1 Paul Bunyan's Country Store
RR 1, Box 57
Blaney Park , MI 49836
906 283-3861
May 1 to Dec.1: Mon. to Sat. 8:30 to 8; Sun. 10 to 8
1 mile north of U.S. 2 on M-77.

GULLIVER

2 Gull's Landing
Gulliver Lake Road
Gulliver, MI 49840
906 283-3373
May 15 to Oct. 15: Mon. to Sat. 10 to 5; evenings by
appointment.
South from U.S. 2 at the blinker light 500 feet, then
right on Gulliver Lake Road; at the Old Deerfield Resort
sign go 1/4 mile down past the Old Deerfield Resort.

MANISTIQUE

3 Phantasmagoria
726 East Lakeshore Drive, Suite 104
Manistique, MI 49854
906 341-6262
Memorial Day weekend to mid-Nov.: Mon. to Fri. 12 to
7, Sat. by chance 12 to 6
In back of a small shopping mall, north side of highway.

4 Christopher's
211 Oak Street
Manistique, MI
906 341-2570
April 1 to Dec 24: Every day 9 to 8;
Winter: Mon. to Sat. 9 to 5
Downtown, just east of the post office.

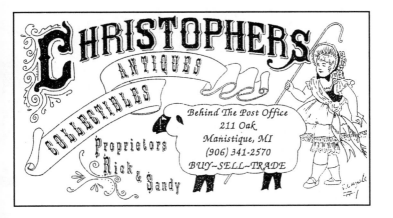

11.05 ALGER COUNTY

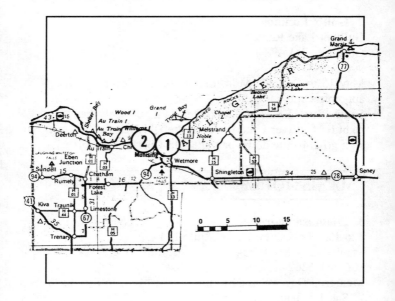

Recommended Points of Interest:
1. Munising: Pictured Rocks National Lakeshore.

Additional Information:
Alger Chamber of Commerce, 906 387±2138

MUNISING

1 The Bay House
111 Elm Avenue
Munising, MI 49862
906 387-4253
Summer: Mon. to Sat. 10 to 7; Sun. 12 to 5
Winter: Tues. to Sat. 10 to 5
Go south at First Peoples Bank.

2 Old North Light Antiques & Gifts
M-28
Munising, MI 49862
906 387-2109
Open 7 days 9 to 9
West of town.
Gifts in front, antiques in back.

11.06 DELTA COUNTY

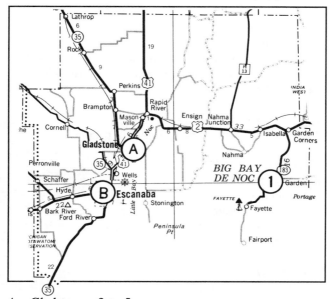

A. Gladstone: 2 to 5
B. Escanaba: 6 to 10

Additional Information:
Delta County Chamber of Commerce, 906 786-2192

GARDEN

1 Antiques in the Garden
MI Route 183
Garden, MI 49835
906 644-2727; 906 644-2348
Memorial Day to Sept. 30: Every day 12 to 5
Downtown   Opened 1993

GLADSTONE

2 Back Stage Antiques
1002 Delta Avenue
Gladstone, MI 49837
906 428-1720
Mon. to Sat. 9:30 to 4:30
West end of downtown in the Rialto Center complex.
Reflections Restaurant next door has antiques for sale.

3 Chicken Coop Antiques
7051 P Road
Gladstone, MI 49837
906 786-1150
May to Nov.: Every Day 12 to 5
From U.S. 41 south of town go east on P Road four blocks; west side of road, just north of 183rd Road. In a shed in back of the house.

4 Fort Wells Antiques
(Bay View Furniture Stripping & Antiques)
7097 P Road
Gladstone, MI 49837
906 786-4264
Year round.
From U.S. 41 south of town go east on P Road two blocks; west side of road across and a block south of The Terrace resort.

5 Foxx Den Antiques
7509 U.S. 2 & 41 & M35
Gladstone , MI 49837
906 786-9014
Tues. to Fri. 10 to 5 other days by chance
West side of highway; in small building in back of the garage, overlooking Bay DeNoc.

ESCANABA

6 Queen's Ransom (formerly Peddlers Alley)
223 Ludington
Escanaba, MI 49826
906 786-8581
Summer: Tues. to Sat. 10 to 6, Sun. 11 to 3;
Winter: Tues. to Sat. 11 to 5, Sun. 11 to 3
Downtown

7 The Market Place
500 Ludington Street
Escanaba, MI 49829
906 789-1326
Mon. to Sat. 10 to 5;
May to Dec. also open Sun. 12:30 to 4
Downtown
Co-op shop; opened 1985; 25 dealers.

8 The Belle Pearl
519 Ludington Street
Escanaba, MI 49829
906 789-0041; 906 786-4919
Mon. to Fri. 11:30 to 5:30; Sat. 11:30 to 3
Downtown, south side of street.

9 Past and Presents
1200 Ludington Street
Escanaba, MI 49829
906 786-1757
Mon. to Sat. 10 to 5
West of downtown, north side of street.
Antiques and hand crafted gifts.

10 U.P. Treasure Hunters Antique Mall
1812 Ludington
Escanaba, MI 49829
No telephone listed.
Open year round, Daily 10 to 6
5 Blocks East of US 2 & 41 Intersection, north side of
street.
12,000 square feet; one of the few malls in the U.P.

See the Calendar of Antique Markets on page 230,
and the Index of Dealer Specialties on page 236.
See the Introduction for an explanation on how this
Directory is organized.   Contact the publisher if
you have any suggestions for improving the content
or format of the Book.

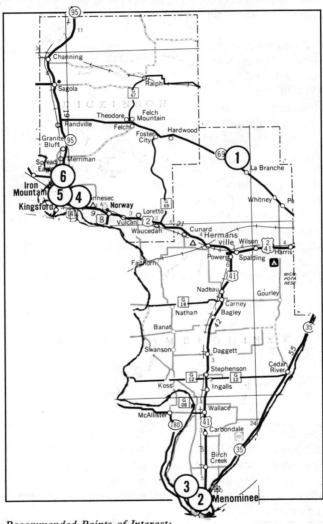

Recommended Points of Interest:

1. Hermansville: IXL Museum, office of lumber mill unchanged in 75 years. 4 blocks south of U.S. 2; June to Aug. 1 to 4 daily; 906 498-2410 or 906 498-2410.
2. Iron Mountain: Cornish Pump and Mining Museum, U.S. 2 to Kent Street exit. May to Oct.; 906 774-1086

Additional Information:

Dickinson County Chamber of Commerce, 906 774-2002
Menominee Chamber of Commerce, 906 863-2679

LA BRANCHE

1   Sheba's Shoppe
Highway 69 West
La Branche,   MI
906 246-3596
Mon. & Tues. or by appointment.
2 miles west of La Branche, north side of highway.

MENOMINEE

2   Simply Charming
111 10th Avenue
Menominee,   MI 49858
906 863-5995
Mon. to Fri. 12 to 5, Sun. 12 to 5;
May to Sept. also Sun. 12 to 4
Crafts, florals, gifts, antiques.

3   Ideal Antiques
N. 145 West Drive
Menominee,   MI 49858
906 863-5918
Mon. to Sat. 10 to 5
North of 18th Avenue, west side of street. Northwest of
downtown.

IRON MOUNTAIN - Dickinson County

4   House of Yesteryear Museum
W-7764 U.S. 2
Iron Mountain,   MI 49801
906 774-0789
June to Sept.: Tues., Thurs., Sat. 10 to 5
East side of town, north side of highway.

5   Carriage Oak Antiques & Gifts
103 West "A" Street
Iron Mountain,   MI 49801
906 774-5777
Mon. to Fri. 10 to 5; Sat. 10 to 3:30
Downtown, 1 block west of U.S. 2, south side of street.
Antiques and gifts.

6 Cobweb Antiques
N-3956 North US-2
Iron Mountain, MI 49801
906 774-6560
Mon. to Sat. 1 to 4, or by appointment.
South of M-95 & U.S. 2 junction, north side of street.

MAP OF MARQUETTE COUNTY:

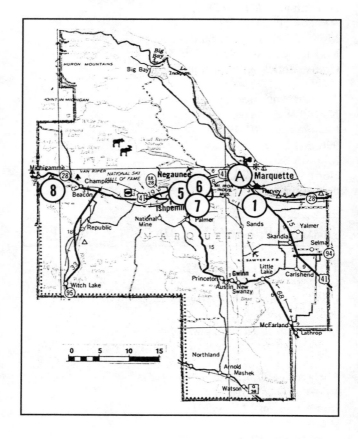

11.09 MARQUETTE COUNTY

MAP ON PRECEDING PAGE

A. Marquette: 2 to 4 (See Detail Map)

Recommended Points of Interest:
1. Negaunee: Michigan Iron Industry Museum, M-35 to County Road 492. 906 475-7857
2. Marquette: Maritime Museum, North Lakeshore Boulevard. Memorial Day to Sept.; 906 226-2006
3. Marquette: Vierling Saloon, 119 South Front at Main Street. 1883 saloon, good view of harbor.

Additional Information:
Marquette County Tourism Council, 906 228-7749.

HARVEY

1 Antique Village
2296 U.S. 41 South
Harvey, MI 49855
906 249-3040
May 1 to Dec. 24: Mon. to Sat. 10 to 6, Sun. 12 to 5
West side of highway, north of M-28 & U.S. 41 junction.

MARQUETTE

2 The Collector Antiques
214 South Front
Marquette, MI 49855
906 228-4134
Mon. to Sat. 10 to 5:30, Sun. 12 to 4
Downtown, west side of street.

3 Fagan's Antiques
219 West Washington
Marquette, MI 49855
906 228-4311
Mon. to Sat. 11 to 5; Sun. by chance
Downtown, south side of street.

Detail map: Marquette

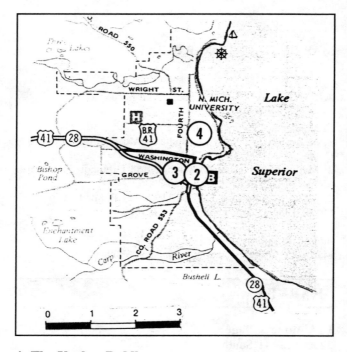

4 The Yankee Peddler
611 North Third Street
Marquette, MI 49855
906 226-2973
Mon. to Fri. 11 to 5, Sat. 11 to 3
North of downtown, east side of street.

NEGAUNEE

5 Old Bank Building Antiques
31 Iron Street,
Negaunee, MI 49866
906 475-4777
Mon. to Sat. 10 to 5, Sun. 12 to 4
Downtown

6 Kate's Collectibles
28 U.S. 41 East
Negaunee, MI 49866
906 475-4443
Open 7 days 10 to 5 year 'round
South side of highway, east of town.

7 The Renovators Antiques
600 U.S. 41 East
Negaunee, MI 49866
906 475-5600
Mon. to Sat. 10 to 6, Sun. 11 to 5
North side of highway at Pine Street.

CHAMPION

8 Michigamme Lake Lodge Gift Shop
U.S. 41
Champion, MI 49814
906 339-4400
May 1 to Oct. 30: Whenever lodge is open.
South side of highway.
Small shop with only a few antiques. The rustic 1934
lodge, however, is worth staying at if at all possible.

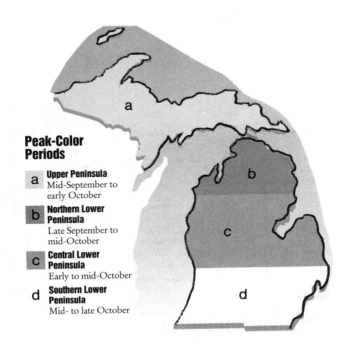

Peak-Color Periods

a Upper Peninsula
Mid-September to early October

b Northern Lower Peninsula
Late September to mid-October

c Central Lower Peninsula
Early to mid-October

d Southern Lower Peninsula
Mid- to late October

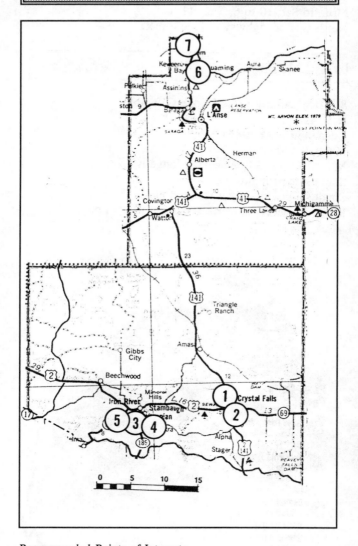

Recommended Points of Interest:
1. Baraga: Hanka Homestead, 1920's Finnish farmstead; U.S. Highway 41 North. 906 353-7116 or 906 334-2590
2. Iron River: Bewabic State Park, and Ski Brule summer and winter sports area.

Additional Information:
Iron County Chamber of Commerce, 906 254-3822

CRYSTAL FALLS

1 Bargain Barn Antiques
1340 West US-2
Crystal Falls, MI 49920
906 875-3381
Thurs. to Mon. 10 to 5
North side of highway, west end of town.

2 Old Tradition Shop
612 Michigan Avenue
Crystal Falls, MI 49920
906 875-4214
Memorial Day to Oct. 1: Every Day 9 to 5;
Winter by chance or appointment.
Southwest of Downtown.

IRON RIVER

3 Apple Orchard Antiques
1603 Kofmehl Road
Iron River, MI 49935
906 265-9723
June 1 to Oct. 1: By chance
From U.S. 2 East go south on Bates Gaastra Road, just
east of a school. Continue two miles; road becomes
Kofmehl Road. East side of road.

4 Ethel Joyce Turbessi at the Antique Cottage
545 West Ice Lake Road
Iron River, MI 49935
906 265-9753 or 906 265-2756
By chance.
South from U.S. 2 at the red & yellow Lakeshore Motel
sign.

5 Sophie's Antiques
101 Meadow View Drive
Iron River, MI 49935
906 265-5978
Sun. 12:30 to 7
2 miles west of town, 2 miles south of U.S. 2, west side
of street.

BARAGA

6 The Country Shop
Rte. 1 Box 66
Baraga, MI 49908
906 353-7230
May to Oct. by chance.
5 miles north of Baraga on Jurmu Road off U.S. 41 on
Keweenaw Bay.
Small house in back of garage.

7. A Chosen Remnant
U.S. 41
Between Baraga and Chassell, MI
June to Dec.
906 523-6159
15 miles north of Baraga, east side of highway.

MAP OF GOGEBIC & ONTONAGON COUNTIES:

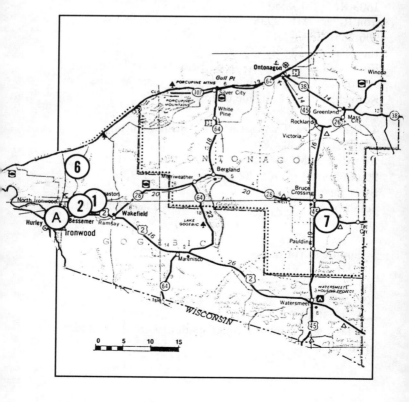

11.12 GOGEBIC COUNTY
11.13 ONTONAGON COUNTY

MAP ON PRECEDING PAGE

A. Ironwood: 3 to 5

Recommended Points of Interest:
1. Ironwood: Black River Drive, scenic 18-mile road; County Road 513 to Lake Superior harbor.
2. Ironwood: Historic buildings, including railroad depot and the Ironwood Theater.
3. Ontonagon: Porcupine Mountains Wilderness State Park, 16 miles west of Ontonagon; 906 885-5275
4. Watersmeet: Sylvania Recreation Area, part of the Ottawa National Forest. The place where the waters from 15 lakes meet.

Additional Information:
Gogebic Area Convention & Visitors Bureau, 906 932-4850.
Ontonagon County Chamber of Commerce, 906 885-5275

RAMSAY

1 U.S. 2 Antiques
U.S. 2 & Blackjack Road
Ramsay, MI
906 667-0642; 906 667-0681
Tues. to Fri. 10 to 5; also Sun. June to Aug.
2 miles east of Bessemer, north side of U.S. 2.

BESSEMER

2 Sellar Street Antiques
114 East Sellar Street
Bessemer, MI 49911
906 667-0191
Mon. Thurs. & Sat. 11 to 4
Downtown, 3 blocks south of U.S. 2.

IRONWOOD

3 The Depot Antiques
316 Lake Street
Ironwood, MI 49938
906 932-0900
Mon. to Sat. 9:30 to 4
East side of Ironwood, a block south of U.S. 2.

4 Doreen's Antiques
313 Lake Street
Ironwood, MI 49938
906 932-4310; res.: 906 932-4933
Mon. to Sat. 10 to 4
West side of Ironwood, a block south of U.S. 2.

5 The Village Store
701 East McLeod Avenue
Ironwood , MI 49938
906 932-5394
Summer: Mon. to Sat. 10:30 to 4; Winter: 11 to 4
From U.S. 2 east of Ironwood go south on Lake Street,
which curves west to become McLeod Avenue; south
side of street.

6 The Net Loft Antiques
Black River Road
Ironwood, MI 49938
906 932-3660
From U.S. 2 east of Ironwood go north on Powderhorn
Road, past Airport Road to Black River Road, north to
Black River Park.

BRUCE CROSSING - Ontonagon County

7 Northern Lights Antiques & Artisans
575 Himanka Hill Road
Bruce Crossing, MI 49912
906 827-3933
May 15 to Sept. 15: Every Day 11 to 5; Winter by
chance.
South on U.S. 45 4 miles from Mich. Route 28, then
east .9 mile. North side of road in brown metal
building.

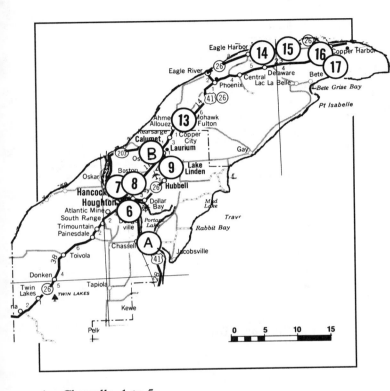

A. Chassell: 1 to 5
B. Calumet: 10 to 12

Recommended Points of Interest:
1. Houghton: A.E. Seaman Mineralogical Museum, 5th floor of Michigan Technological University Electrical Energy Resources Center. 906 487-2572
2. Calumet: Shute's 1890 Bar, 322 Sixth Street.
3. Copper Harbor: Keweenaw Mountain Lodge, U.S. 41 South; rustic restaurant & cottages.
4. Copper Harbor: Fort Wilkins Historic Complex, U.S. 41 East; 1843 Army outpost. 906 289-4215
5. Isle Royal National Park: The boat from Copper Harbor is a 56 mile ride. Facilities are open from mid-June to mid-October.

Additional Information:
Keweenaw Tourism Council, 906 482-2388

CHASSELL

1 Eagle Shop
148 N. Wilson Drive (U.S. 41)
Chassell, MI 49916
906 523-4423
May 1 to Oct. 30: Mon. to Sat. 9:30 to 5:30
North end of town, west side of highway.

2 Grandma's Antiques
300 Wilson Memorial Drive (U.S. 41)
Chassell, MI 49916
No telephone listed.
By chance.
West side of street.
Piled high with stuff.

3 Pine Cone Shop
308 Wilson Memorial Drive (U.S. 41)
Chassell, MI 49916
906 523-4309
May 1 to Oct. 31: Mon. to Sat. 9:30 to 5
West side of street.

4 Einerlei Shop
422 Wilson Memorial Drive (US 41)
Chassell, MI 49916
906 523-4612
Winter: Mon. to Sat. 10-5, Sun. 11-5
Summer: Mon. to Sat. 9-6, Sun. 11-5
West side of the street.
Gifts, home furnishings, herb garden, some antiques.

5 Porch Antiques
447 U.S. 41
Chassell, MI 49916
906 523-4819
Mar. 1 to Dec.1: Mon. to Sat. 10 to 5
West side of highway, north side of town.

Also See: **A Chosen Rmenant**, located on U.S. 41
south of Chassell & north of Baraga, on page 222.

HOUGHTON

6 Antique Mall
418 Sheldon Avenue
Houghton, MI 49931
906 487-9483
June 1 to Sept. 1: Mon. to Fri. 10 to 6, Sat. 10 to 5;
(May be closing in late 1994)
Downtown

HANCOCK

7 Northwoods Trading Post
120 Quincy
Hancock, MI 49930
906 482-5210
Mon. to Thurs. 9:30 to 5:30; Fri. 9:30 to 6; Sat. 9:30 to 5
Downtown south side of street.
Antiques and collectibles and some furniture.

8 Grapevine Resale Shop
129 Quincy
Hancock, MI 49930
906 482-0104
Mon. to Fri. 10 to 5:30, Sat. 11 to 4
Downtown, north side of street
Vintage clothing, collectibles.

LAKE LINDEN

9 Treasured Friends Antiques
313 Calumet Street
Lake Linden, MI 49945
906 296-0184; res.: 906 296-0604
July & Aug.: Mon. to Sat. 12:30 to 4:30

CALUMET

10 Copper World
101 Fifth Street
Calumet, MI 49913
906 337-4016
July 4 to Labor Day: Mon. to Sat. 9 to 8;
Winter: Mon. to Sat. 9:30 to 5
Downtown;   New and old copper items.

11 Del's Antiques
308 Fifth Street, Downtown
Calumet, MI 49913
906 337-3972
May to Oct.: Mon. to Sat. 12 to 5

12 The Rose & The Thorn
451 Pine
Calumet, MI 49913
906 337-1717
May to Oct.: Mon. to Fri. 9 - 9, Sat. 9 - 5, Sun. 12 - 5;
Winter: Mon. to Sat. 10 - 5, Sun. by chance
North end of downtown; NEC 5th & Pine Streets.
Ceramics & gifts 1st floor, antiques in basement.

ALLOUEZ - Keweenaw County

13 The Last Place on Earth
U.S. 41
Allouez, MI 49805
906 337-1014
May 1 to Oct. 15: Every Day 9 to 5
West side of highway, 3 miles north of Calumet.

EAGLE HARBOR

14 The Museum Shop
Route 1 Box 190
Eagle Harbor, MI 49950
906 289-4911
May 27 to Sept. 30: Mon. to Sat. 10 to 6, Sun. 2 to 5
North side of highway, east side of town, on the grounds
of the Eagle Harbor Light House.
Specializing in copper items and Victorian transferware.

PHONE (906) 289-4913

Chit Chat Antiques

AND COLLECTIBLES

LOIS AND GEORGE ELGH
24 SAND DUNES DRIVE
EAGLE HARBOR, MI 49950

MON THRU SAT. 10-5
SUN 12-5

15 Chit Chat Antiques & Collectibles
24 Sand Dunes Road
Eagle Harbor, MI 49950
906 289-4913
Mon. to Sat. 10 to 5, Sun. 12 to 5
Just north on MI Route 26.

COPPER HARBOR

16 Log Cabin Gifts
MI Route 26
Copper Harbor, MI 49918
906 289-4560
June 1 to Sept. 1: Every Day 10 to 6
South side of road, 4 miles west of Copper Harbor.

17 Minnetonka's Aster House Museum
U.S. 41 & MI Route 26
Copper Harbor, MI
906 289-4449
May 15 to Oct. 15: Every day 9 to 6
Center of town.
Antique shop & museum in back of the motel.

ANTIQUE MARKETS IN EASTERN MICHIGAN: JUNE 1994 TO MAY 1995

The following calendar of selected antique markets was prepared in April 1994. Be aware that times may change and some shows may be cancelled; call to confirm dates and times.

JUNE 1994

Thurs. to Sun. June 2 to 5: Orchard Mall Antique Show, Orchard Mall, Orchard Lake & Maple, West Bloomfield. Thurs. to Sat. 10 to 9; Sun. 12 to 5. 313 548-9066

Thurs. to Sun. June 2 to 5: Meridian Mall Antique Show, Meridian Mall, Grand River at Marsh, Okemos. Thurs. to Sat. 10 to 9, Sun. 12 to 5. 616 629-3133

Sat. & Sun. June 4 & 5: 3rd Annual Red Cross Collectibles & Craft Market, Washtenaw Farm Council Grounds, Ann Arbor-Saline Road, Ann Arbor. Sat. 9 to 5 Sun. 11 to 4. Admission: $2.00. 810 971-5300

Sat. & Sun. June 4 & 5: Grosse Pointe Christ Church Antique Show, the High School, Grosse Pointe. Sat. 10 to 6; Sun. 12 to 5. Admission: $5.00. 313 885-4841

Sat. & Sun. June 4 & 5: Michigan Antique Festival, Midland Fairgrounds, U.S. 10 & Eastman Road, Midland. Sat. 8 to 7; Sun. 8 to 4. Admission: $3.00. 517 687-9001

Sat. & Sun. June 4 & 5: Sporting Collectibles Show, Midland Holiday Inn, 1500 West Wackerly, Midland. Admission: $3.00. 616 879-3912

Fri. to Sun. June 10 to 12: Gibraltar Antique & Collectible Show, Gibraltar Trade Center, 227 N. River Road, Mt. Clemens. Admission: $1.50 per car load. 810 465-6440

Sun. June 19: Brusher Ann Arbor Antique Market, 5055 Ann Arbor-Saline Road, I-94 Exit 175, Ann Arbor. Sun. 6 to 4. Admission: $4.00. 313 662-9453

Sun. June 19: Belleville Antiques Market, Fairgrounds, 10871 Quirk Road, I-94 Exit 190, Belleville. Admission: $3.00. 616 679-2131

Thurs. to Sun. June 23 to 26: Courtland Mall Antique Show, Flint. Thurs. to Sat. 10 to 9, Sun. 12 to 5. 616 445-8790

Sat. June 25: The 2nd Annual Antique Market & Strawberry Festival, Sashabaw Presbyterian Church, 5300 Maybee Road, Clarkston. Sat. 8 to 4. Admission: Free. 810 673-3101

JULY 1994
Sat. & Sun. July 2 & 3: Superfest Collectors Event, Washtenaw Farm Council Grounds, Ann Arbor-Saline Road, Saline. Sat. 8 to 6 Sun. 9 to 4. Admission: $3.00. 517 676-2079

Sat. & Sun. July 2 & 3: Chelsea Antiques Market, Chelsea Fairgrounds, I-94 Exit 159, North to light then left, Chelsea. Sat. 7 to 6 Sun. 8 to 4. Admission: $4.00. 517 456-6153

Mon. July 4: Outdoor Flea Market, Next to the Hitching Post Antiques Mall, M-50 & M-52, Tecumseh. Mon. 6 to 4. Admission: Free. 517 423-8277

Sat. & Sun. July 9 & 10: Utica Antiques Market, Knights of Columbus Grounds, 21 Mile Road, east of Van Dyke, Utica. Sat. 7 to 6, Sun. 8 to 4. Admission: $4.00. 517 456-6153

Sunday July 10: Doll Show, Van Dyke Park Suite Hotel, 31800 Van Dyke, Warren. Sun. 10 to 4. Admission: $2.50. 810 757-5568

Sunday July 10: Antiques at Domino's Farms of Ann Arbor, Domino's Farms, 24 Frank Lloyd Wright Drive, Ann Arbor. Sun. 8 to 4. Admission: $3.00, Parking Free. 616 679-213

Fri. to Sun. July 15 to 17: St. Clair Riverview Mall Antique Show & Sale, along St. Clair River across from St. Clair Inn, St. Clair. Fri. & Sat. 9 to 9, Sun. 10 to 5. 313 487-5078

Sat. & Sun. July 23 & 24: Michigan Antique Festival, Midland Fairgrounds, U.S. 10 & Eastman Road, Midland. Sat. 8 to 7; Sun. 8 to 4. Admission: $3.00. 517 687-9001

AUGUST 1994
Thurs. to Sun. Aug. 18 to 21: Universal Mall Antique Show, Warren. Thurs. to Sat. 10 to 9, Sun. 12 to 5. 616 445-8790

Thurs. to Sun. Aug. 24 to 27: Crosswinds Mall Antique Show, Orchard Lake Road at Lone Pine (17 Mile) Rd., West Bloomfield. Thurs. to Sat. 10 to 9, Sun. 12 to 5. 810 851-7630

Thurs. to Sun. Aug. 24 to 27: Westwood Mall Antique Show, Jackson. Thurs. to Sat. 10 to 9, Sun. 12 to 5. 616 445-8790

SEPTEMBER 1994
Sat. to Mon., Sept. 3 to 5: Chesaning Antiques Festival, On the Boulevard, Chesaning. 10 to 6. Admission: Free. 517 845-7775

Mon. Sept. 5: Outdoor Flea Market, Next to the Hitching

Post Antiques Mall, M-50 & M-52, Tecumseh. Mon. 6 to 4. Admission: Free. 517 423-8277

Sat. & Sun. Sept. 10 & 11: Utica Antiques Market, Knights of Columbus Grounds, 21 Mile Road, east of Van Dyke, Utica Sat. 7 to 6 Sun. 8 to 4. Admission: $4.00. 517 456-6153

Sat. & Sun. Sept, 10 & 11: Great Lakes Collector's Showcase, E A Cummings Center, 6135 E Mt. Morris, Flint. Sat. & Sun. 8 to 5. 616 629-3133

Sat. & Sun. Sept. 10 & 11: Spring Antique Festival, Williamston. Sat. 9 to 6, Sun. 10 to 4. 517 676-9227 or 517 655-2622

Sun. Sept. 11: Antiques at Domino's Farms of Ann Arbor, Domino's Farms, 24 Frank Lloyd Wright Drive, Ann Arbor. Sun. 8 to 4. Admission: $3.00, Parking Free. 616 679-2131

Sun. Sept. 11: Doll Show & Sale, Knights of Columbus Hall, 4840 Shattuck, Saginaw. 10 to 4. Admission: $3.00. 517 684-6891

Thurs. to Sun. Sept. 15 to 18: Great Northern Show, Genessee Valley Mall, Flint. 616 629-3133

Thurs. to Sun. Sept. 15 to 18: Macomb Mall Antique Show, Roseville. Thurs. to Sat. 10 to 9, Sun. 12 to 5. 616 445-8790

Sat. & Sun. Sept. 17 & 18: Superfest Collectors Event, Monroe Co. Fairground, M-50 between bet. I-75 & US-23 Monroe. Sat. 8 to 6 Sun. 9 to 4. Admission: $3.00. 517 676-2079

Sun. Sept. 18: Doll Show, Van Dyke Park Suite Hotel, 31800 Van Dyke, Warren. Sun. 10 to 4. $2.50. 810 757-5568

Fri. to Sun. Sept. 23 to 25: Autumn Antiques Show, Novi Expo Center; I-96 at Exit 162 (Novi Road) west of I-696, Novi. Admission: $5.00. 517 626-6432

Fri. to Sun. Sept. 23 to 25: Southfield Pavilion Antique Exposition, Southfield Civic Center, Southfield. Fri. 2 to 9, Sat. 12 to 8, Sun. 12 to 5. Admission: $5.00. 810 469-1706

Sat. & Sun. Sept. 24 & 25: Michigan Antique Festival, Midland Fairgrounds, U.S. 10 & Eastman Road, Midland. Sat. 8 to 7; Sun. 8 to 4. Admission: $3.00. 517 687-9001

Sat. & Sun. Sept 24 & 25: Antique & Design Fall Festival, Grand Hotel, Mackinac Island. Sat. 12 to 5, Sun. 10 to 12. Admission: $5.00. 800 33-GRAND; 517 349-4600

Sun. Sept. 25: Springfield Oaks Antique Show and Sale, Oakland Park Youth Activity Building, 12451 S. Andersonville Road, Davison. Sun. 9 to 4. Free. 810 623-9014

Sept. 29 - Oct. 2: Great Northern Show, Meridian Mall, Lansing/Okemos. 616 629-3133

OCTOBER 1994
Sat. & Sun. Oct. 1 & 2: Chelsea Antiques Market, Chelsea Fairgrounds, I-94 Exit 159, Chelsea. Sat. 7 to 6 Sun. 8 to 4. Admission: $4.00. 517 456-6153

Thurs. to Sun. Oct. 6 to 9: Arborland Mall Antique Show, Ann Arbor. Thurs. to Sat. 10 to 9, Sun. 12 to 5. 616 445-8790

Sun. Oct. 9: Michigan Antiquarian Book and Paper Show, New Lansing Center, 333 East Michigan Ave., Lansing. 10 to 5. Admission: $3.00. 517 332-1915

Sat. & Sun. Oct. 15 & 16: Superfest Collectors Event, Ingham County Fairgrounds, Mason. Sat. 8 to 6, Sun. 9 to 4. Admission: $3.00. 517 676-2079

Sat. & Sun. Oct. 15 & 16: J.C. Wyno Antique & Collectible Show, Dearborn Civic Center, 15801 Michigan Av. Dearborn. Sat. 10 to 6 Sun. 10 to 4. Admission: $2.50. 810 772-2253

Thurs. to Sun. Oct. 20 to 23: Adrian Mall Antique Show, Adrian. Thurs. to Sat. 10 to 9, Sun. 12 to 5. 616 445-8790

Sat. & Sun. Oct. 22 & 23: Bluewater Antique Dealers Association, St. Clair County Community College, Port Huron. Sat. 10 to 6; Sun. 10 to 5.

Sun. Oct. 30: Springfield Oaks Antique Show and Sale, Oakland Park Youth Activity Building, 12451 S. Andersonville Road, Davison. Sun. 9 to 4. Free. 810 623-9014

NOVEMBER 1994
Thurs. to Sun. Nov. 3 to 6: Crosswinds Mall Antique Show, Orchard Lake Rd. at Lone Pine (17 Mile) Road, West Bloom-field. Thurs. to Sat. 10 to 9, Sun. 12 to 5. 810 851-7630

Sun. Nov. 6: Doll Show, Van Dyke Park Suite Hotel, 31800 Van Dyke, Warren. Sun. 10 to 4. Admission: $2.50. 810 757-5568

Fri. to Sun. Nov. 18 to 20: Southfield Americana Antiques Show & Sale, Southfield Civic Center, Southfield. Fri. 2 to 9, Sat. 12 to 8, Sun. 12 to 5. Admission: $5.00. 810 469-1706

Sat. & Sun. Nov. 26 & 27: J.C. Wyno Antique & Collectible Show, Dearborn Civic Center, 15801 Michigan Av. Dearborn. Sat. 10 to 6 Sun. 10 to 4. Admission: $2.50. 810 772-2253

Sat. & Sun. Nov. 26 & 27: Great Northern Antique Show, Lansing Center, Lansing. 616 629-3133

Sun. Nov. 27: Springfield Oaks Antique Show and Sale, Oakland Park Youth Activity Building, 12451 S. Andersonville Road, Davison. Sun. 9 to 4. Free. 810 623-9014

DECEMBER 1994

Sunday Dec. 4: Doll Show, Van Dyke Park Suite Hotel, 31800 Van Dyke, Warren. Sun. 10 to 4. Admission: $2.50. 810 757-5568

Sat. & Sun. Dec. 10 & 11: Winter Antiques Market, Univ. of Michigan Sports Coliseum, I-94 exit 175 north, Ann Arbor. Sat. 8 to 6 Sun. 9 to 4. Admission: $4.00. 517 456-6153

Sat. & Sun. Dec. 31 & Jan. 1: Winter Antiques Market, University of Michigan Sports Coliseum, Ann Arbor. Sat. 8 to 6 Sun. 9 to 4. Admission: $4.00. 517 456-6153

JANUARY 1995

Sun. Jan, 22: Springfield Oaks Antique Show and Sale, Oakland Park Youth Activity Building, 12451 S. Andersonville Road, Davison. Sun. 9 to 4. Free. 810 623-9014

Fri. & Sat. Jan. 20 & 21: St. James Church Winter Antiques Show, 355 W Maple Road, Birmingham. Fri. 10 to 9 Sat. 10 to 5. Admission: $5.00. 810 644-0820

FEBRUARY 1995

Sat. & Sun. Feb. 4 & 5: The Dearborn Historic Guild Antique Show & Sale, Civic Center, Dearborn. Sat. 10 to 8, Sun. 10 to 5. Admission: $3.00. 313 565-3000

Sat. & Sun. Feb. 18 & 19: Winter Antiques Market Univ. of Michigan Sports Coliseum, Ann Arbor. Sat. 8 to 6 Sun. 9 to 4. Admission: $4.00. 517 456-6153

Fri. to Sun. Feb. 24 to 26: Southfield Pavilion Antique Exposition, Southfield Civic Center, Southfield. Fri. 2 to 9, Sat. 12 to 8, Sun. 12 to 5. Admission: $5.00. 810 469-1706

Sun. Feb. 26: Springfield Oaks Antique Show and Sale, Oakland Park Youth Activity Building, 12451 S. Andersonville Road, Davison. Sun. 9 to 4. Admission free. 810 623-9014

MARCH 1995
Fri. to Sun. March 10 to 12: Spring Antiques Show, Novi
Expo Center; I-96 at Exit 162 (Novi Road) west of I-696,
Novi. Admission: $5.00. 517 626-6432

Fri. to Sun. March 24 to 26: The Southfield Americana
Antiques Show, Southfield Civic Center, Southfield. Fri. 2 to
9, Sat. 12 to 8, Sun. 12 to 5. $5.00. 313 469-1706

Sun. March 26: Springfield Oaks Antique Show and Sale,
Oakland Park Youth Activity Building, 12451 S. Andersonville
Road, Davison. Sun. 9 to 4. Free. 810 623-9014

APRIL 1995
Sat. & Sun. April 8 & 9: Chelsea Antiques Market, Chelsea
Fairgrounds, I-94 Exit 159, North to light then left, Chelsea.
Sat. 7 to 6 Sun. 8 to 4. Admission: $4.00. 517 456-6153

Sat. & Sun. April 14 & 15: Southeastern Mich. Antique Sporting Collectibles Show; Weber's Inn, Ann Arbor. Sat. 1 to 9,
Sun. 9 to 4. Admission: $5.00. 616 879-3912

Sun. April 23: Springfield Oaks Antique Show and Sale,
Oakland Park Youth Activity Building, 12451 S. Andersonville
Road, Davison. Sun. 9 to 4. Free. 810 623-9014

Sat. & Sun. April 28 & 29: Southfield Modernism Exposition;
Southfield Civic Center, Southfield. Sat. 11 to 9, Sun. 12 to 5.
Admission: likely to be $6.00. 810 469-17706

MAY 1995
Sat. & Sun. May 13 & 14: Utica Antiques Market, Knights of
Columbus Grounds, 21 Mile Road, east of Van Dyke, Utica.
Sat. 7 to 6 Sun. 8 to 4. Admission: $4.00. 517 456-6153

Fri. to Sun. May. 25 to 27: Spring Antiques Show, Novi
Expo Center; I-96 at Exit 162 (Novi Road) west of I-696,
Novi. Admission: $5.00 517 626-6432

Monday May 29: Outdoor Flea Market, Next to the Hitching
Post Antiques Mall, M-50 & M-52, Tecumseh. Mon. 6 to 4.
Admission: Free. 517 423-8277

NOTE: SOME ANTIQUE SHOW
MANAGERS WILL GIVE A
REDUCED ADMISSION FEE
UPON SHOWING YOUR COPY OF
THE COMPLETE ANTIQUE SHOP DIRECTORY

INDEX OF DEALER SPECIALTIES

Index of Dealer Specialties - continued

A MESSAGE FROM THE PUBLISHER

ANTIQUE COLLECTORS: I hope you find this Directory helpful as you search for the antiques you are interested in. If you come upon any new shops, or if you find changes or errors in the listings, please let me know.

You can help assure that this series of Antique Shop Directories is continued and updated annually. When you visit a shop, tell the dealer you read about his or her shop in the *Complete Antique Shop Directory*.

Also, please make a special effort to support those dealers who have supported the publication of this Directory: Visit those shops with a Display Ad.

Thank you.

Edward Lawrence, Publisher
Complete Antique Shop Directories
14906 Red Arrow Highway
Lakeside, Michigan 49116
616 469-5995